The Leadership Lifecycle

THE LEADERSHIP LIFECYCLE

Matching Leaders to Evolving Organizations

Andrew Ward

palgrave
macmillan

First published 2003 by
PALGRAVE MACMILLAN
Houndmills, Basingstoke, Hampshire RG21 6XS and
175 Fifth Avenue, New York, N.Y. 10010
Companies and representatives throughout the world

PALGRAVE MACMILLAN is the global academic imprint of the Palgrave Macmillan division of St. Martin's Press, LLC and of Palgrave Macmillan Ltd. Macmillan® is a registered trademark in the United States, United Kingdom and other countries. Palgrave is a registered trademark in the European Union and other countries.

ISBN 0–333–99362–4 hardback

This book is printed on paper suitable for recycling and made from fully managed and sustained forest sources.

A catalogue record for this book is available from the British Library.

A catalog record for this book is available from the Library of Congress.

Editing and origination by Aardvark Editorial, Mendham, Suffolk

10 9 8 7 6 5 4 3 2 1
12 11 10 09 08 07 06 05 04 03

Printed and bound in Great Britain by
Creative Print & Design (Wales), Ebbw Vale

CONTENTS

PREFACE

Each year dozens of biographies of great leaders across an array of different fields are published. Each has a fascinating story which is unique in its own way. Yet for decades, even centuries, scholars of organizations and practitioners alike have sought to codify the characteristics and skills of a great leader. In many respects, the work for this book started out with the same quest. I have long been fascinated by biographies and tales of great heroic leadership, particularly in the context of business organizations, and in drawing general lessons from these accounts that may have wider application for leaders. However, one can't escape the fact that each of these lives is essentially embedded in a particular context. Each successful leader has led in a way that was right for the unique situation that he or she faced at the time. Given different circumstances and different times some of these same leaders would either lead differently or perhaps even fail in their leadership.

Thus, the more I studied these great leaders of the past and present, the more obvious it became that one cannot look at the leader in isolation for an example of great leadership, but must in fact look at the leader in conjunction with the situation, and in particular at the fit between the leader's actions and style and the context in which those actions take place.

At first glance, this complication would seem to render the search for an ideal leader hopeless, as each situation faced is surrounded by its own set of circumstances. However, while this implies that there is no one ideal leadership type that fits all situations, within an organizational context at least, there are sufficiently strong and predictable commonalities to indicate an ideal type for each of these organizational circumstances. The framework that I use to categorize the different organizational contexts has largely come about through my teaching the leadership course at Goizueta Business School over the last several years. In teaching this course I have invited many leaders of business, government, and non-profit organizations to speak to my class about what leadership means in their organization and the challenges they face. As one listens to these leaders, and particularly the same leaders across different years, it becomes apparent that the leadership needs in their organizations change over time. Also apparent is that many organizations face similar challenges at about the same point in their existence. This observation gave rise to the central thesis of this book – that an organization's leadership needs to change over time, but change systematically to match the current requirements of the organization.

One major corollary of this central thesis is that as the leadership role in organizations changes, the leader him- or herself may or may not be able to make the required transition. As such, leaders, who have been successful at leading their organizations in the past, suddenly find themselves less able to lead and often see their organizations go into decline in spite of, and indeed precisely because of, the fact that they have continued with their own tried and true leadership style. During the course of writing my Ph.D. dissertation several years ago entitled "The harder they fall? What happens to CEOs who are fired?", I spent the better part of a year traveling to various parts of the country interviewing dethroned chief executives, and board members who had fired their CEO. In between blaming their exit on political struggles and Machiavellian plots to overthrow them, time and time again I would hear tales from ousted CEOs of how the environment had changed on them and how the board had been too quick to get rid of them before their changed course had had time to take effect. From the other side of the boardroom, I would hear that the environment had indeed changed and the board no longer considered the CEO to be the right person to lead the company forward. The company had moved from one phase of its lifecycle to the next, its leadership needs had shifted, and the CEO was unable to adapt along with it.

This book then serves as a cautionary tale for organizations, their leaders, the boards that appoint those leaders and indeed everyone in the organization who ultimately feels the fallout when organizations fail. Organizations do change in fundamental ways as they traverse their lifecycle, and as they change, the required leadership role correspondingly changes, and in ways that many leaders find hard to adjust to. However, this tale has hope as well as caution in that it enables organizations and those that lead them to identify when these changes occur and what adjustments need to be made to navigate the transition in lifestage successfully. Many leaders are able to guide themselves and their organizations successfully through these turbulent waters to smoother sailing in the next lifestage, but it takes recognition of the need to fundamentally change the leadership role as the organization makes this transition.

While this book is about leadership in organizations, it is not solely confined to the top executive suite. Leadership occurs, and is necessary, at all levels of the organization, and just as the fit between the leadership role and the organization is vital at the top, it is equally applicable for leadership roles in divisions, groups and teams throughout the organization. Indeed, for leaders at the lower levels of the organization, the fit between the leadership role and the organization is often complicated by the different lifestage of the group to that of the organization as a whole. In such cases, the leader needs to be aware of the implications of the different lifestages and how his or her leadership role in the group fits with the overall organization and consequences for the leader's career progression through the organization. As such, this book has as vital a message for leaders and aspiring leaders at all levels of the organization as it does for those at the top.

ANDREW WARD
Atlanta, GA

ACKNOWLEDGMENTS

You often hear laments about the loneliness of writing a book. I have found the opposite to be true. Writing a book such as this demands the involvement of, and interaction with, many people and so there are a lot of people to whom I owe a debt of gratitude. Indeed, the process of writing this book really began almost a decade ago and so I am bound to omit many of the people to whom I owe thanks – hopefully they will forgive me.

First, I wish to thank Jeffrey Sonnenfeld and everyone at the Chief Executive Leadership Institute (formerly the Center for Leadership & Career Studies) for their contributions over the years, both directly and indirectly, in making this endeavor possible. Without them I would not have even been in a position to write this book.

Beyond this singular contribution, there are a host of people who have assisted with research, refining, editing and access; among them are: Ido Alexander, Jorge Casimiro, Jeff Cohn, Roshan Dharia, Michael Feder, Brandon Fishman, David Fraser, Mary Fraser, Susan Glenn, Liz Hamilton, Joyce Joseph, Priti Lokre, Bob Lussier, Chris Mangum, Nadia Munasifi, Arathi Narasimhan, Jennifer Pendergast, Bill Roberti, Jason Rosenbaum, Paula Schwed, Rick Smith, Sarah Smith, Julie Stephenson, Ilana Straznik, Leslie Tessler, Helen Waite, John White, and Allison Yazdian. A special measure of thanks for research goes to Leanne Toler. Earnest thanks are also due to the incredible research staff at the Goizueta Business School Library and the Woodruff Library Special Collections division, who were enormously helpful, patient, and always friendly in providing assistance. From Palgrave Macmillan, Stephen Rutt and Jacky Kippenberger have provided expert guidance through the publication process and made it very easy, allowing me to focus on completing the book.

Finally, I would most like to thank all my family, friends and colleagues who have had to bear with me and suffered from my less-than-perfect attention while my efforts have been focused on writing this book. Bearing the brunt of this of course, and yet always with total support, were my wife Sally and our son Samuel, who are no doubt much relieved that it is finally finished. DisneyWorld, here we come!

The author and publishers wish to thank the following for permission to reproduce copyright material:

CMP Media LLC for multiple quotes and excerpts from the August 25 1997 issue of *CRN* (formerly *Computer Reseller News*) reproduced with permission in Chapter 8.

Harvard Business Review for multiple quotes and excerpts reproduced with permission in Chapter 4.

Every effort has been made to trace all the copyright holders but if any have been inadvertently overlooked the publishers will be pleased to make the necessary arrangements at the first opportunity.

CHAPTER 1

The Leadership Lifecycle

We are all endowed with certain inalienable rights …
You have the right to apply for a fishing license … from your home … at 3.15 in the morning.
You have the right to not miss an entire workday … just to renew a driver's license.
You have the right to attend a town meeting … in your underwear.[1]

This was the synopsis of the idea behind govWorks, portrayed in the documentary movie, *Startup.com*, which captured the era of the internet boom and bust in its portrayal of the rapid rise and fall of govWorks. govWorks was conceived to provide a valuable service to consumers, and local governments, by facilitating the often irritating transactions between them; transactions totaling over $600 billion annually. Founded in May 1999, Kaleil Isaza Tuzman and Tom Herman, friends since their high school days, rapidly built the organization and launched an internet portal to allow their vision of easy interaction with government. However, shortly after launch the rapid growth of the organization and difficulties scaling the business sent govWorks on a downward spiral and forced the sale of the business assets to eONE Global on January 1, 2001, a mere 18 months after the founding of the company.

BigWords was another one of the great ideas of the internet boom. Like many of the great ideas of the late 1990s, BigWords' idea rested on the power of the internet to disaggregate a large market. If there was one thing the internet did, it was to enable consumers to obtain more information more easily than ever before. This led to a revolution in business, and spelled danger to the behemoths who relied on limited consumer knowledge or alternatives to uphold mini-monopolies. One such constrained market was the college textbook market. High margins were afforded by essentially local monopolies on individual college campuses – the campus bookstore. Effectively, it was the only place for students to purchase textbooks. In 1998, 23-year-old entrepreneur Matt Johnson founded BigWords to disaggregate this multi-billion dollar market and sell college textbooks over the internet, following much the same model pioneered by Amazon.com in the retail book market. Beginning in the fall semester of 1998, with $75,000 scraped together from friends and family, BigWords began a successful launch selling $12,000 worth of textbooks. In the next semester, January 1999, sales rocketed to $500,000. January 2000 saw $15 million in revenues. In October 2000, two years and 400,000 customers since its founding, BigWords filed for bankruptcy, having attracted and burned through $70 million of venture capital. *Wired* magazine commented that "no one is more emblematic of the ride from Internet euphoria to Internet depression than Matt Johnson."[2]

Two great ideas. Two failures losing well over one hundred million of investors' dollars. Why did they, and hundreds of companies like them, fail? Much has recently been written about the dot-com bubble and its bursting. It is an easy explanation that too much money was thrown at too young entrepreneurs with half-baked ideas. That greed drove the market until fear took over in April 2000, and so the worlds of dot-com entrepreneurs crashed around them, as, through no fault of their own, the market turned against them and cash dried up.

Sure, there is some truth there, and there were some bad calls made, and some people played wild and loose, gambling on very uncertain outcomes with other people's money. But among all the frenzy of the internet bust, there were some genuinely good business ideas which still failed. Was their failure just due to the fallout from the general bust, or was it something more fundamental?

We see the shocking figures of business failure rates from the dot-com bubble, and yet somehow often forget that high failure rates existed for entrepreneurial businesses before we had heard of the internet. Back in the 1970s and 80s, statistics show that one out of every two new businesses failed within the first two years of their existence, and four out of five collapsed within the first five years.[3] So business failure, especially among small entrepreneurial companies, is nothing new, and therefore not something we can just put down to the bursting of the dot-com bubble. So what is the cause of this high level of failure? A Bank of America study concluded that 90% of small business failures were due to managerial incompetence.[4] And before those who lead or work in larger businesses breathe a sigh of relief that such pessimistic conclusions are confined to small, vulnerable companies, pause to digest these statistics: Of the companies listed in the Fortune 500 in 1970, a full third had disappeared by 1993,[5] and in 2001 alone, ten Fortune 500 companies, and 22 Fortune 1000 companies filed for bankruptcy.[6]

So why do companies of all sizes remain vulnerable to failure? The Bank of America survey mentioned above places the blame on incompetent management. However, these are generally the very same managers who have successfully built the organization to start with. What changes management competence to incompetence? The answer lies in the Leadership Lifecycle. As an organization travels through its existence, it goes through identifiable lifestages, which are metaphorically akin to a biological lifecycle. At each of these lifestages, as we shall see, there is a different leadership role which is appropriate for the organization in order for it to sustain itself and prosper, hence the Leadership Lifecycle represents the fit between the leadership role and the organizational lifecycle which enables the organization to succeed.

Organizations, just as products do on a smaller scale, go through a natural lifecycle. Daniel Levinson and colleagues, in the groundbreaking work, *The Seasons of a Man's Life*,[7] describe the male human adult lifecycle and how people make the sometimes difficult transitions from childhood and adolescence to early adulthood; or from early to mid-adulthood or from mid- to late adulthood. Just as humans have distinct phases in their lifecycle, and difficulties in making the transitions between phases, the same is true for organizations. This notion of an organizational lifecycle is not a new one. In 1914, Chapman and Ashton, two academics, contended that:

> the growth of a business and the volume and form which it ultimately assumes are apparently determined in somewhat the same fashion as the development of an organism in the animal or vegetable world. As there is a normal size and form for a man, so, but less markedly, are there normal sizes and forms for a business.[8]

Almost seven decades later, John Kimberly and Bob Miles, two researchers from Yale and Harvard universities, gathered some of the leading academics to contribute to a book titled *The Organizational Lifecycle*[9] which sought to encourage academic researchers to take account of what practitioners already knew – that organizations were dynamic and constantly changing, and that the variations caused by organizations being in different stages of their lifecycle were important. However, while academic researchers continued to pay relatively little attention to the lifecycle of organizations and its implications, despite the call from Kimberly and

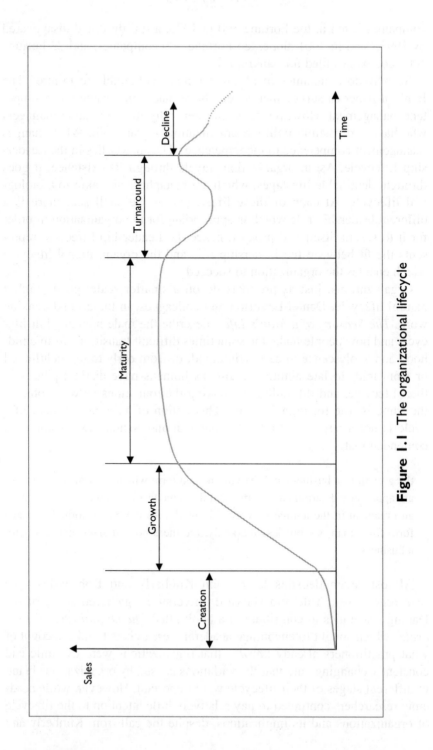

Figure 1.1 The organizational lifecycle

Miles, by living the daily demands of their role, leaders of organizations inherently understand that organizations and their subsequent needs do, in fact, change over time and go through distinct stages in their existence.

The metaphor of the biological lifecycle is useful in describing organizations, as they, like biological lifeforms, have a creation or birth, a period of growth, maturity and decline and finally death. The events and circumstances of birth and early life can shape the development and lifecycle in significant ways for both biological lifeforms and organizations. Certainly there are differences between an organizational lifecycle and a biological lifecycle, such that we use the term "organizational lifecycle" knowing that it is only a metaphor for describing organizations and not an exact replica of the biological lifecycle. For instance, for biological lifeforms, death is an inevitable consequence of living, whereas for organizations, this might not necessarily be so. Because death is inevitable for the biological form, for any particular species, there is a typical lifecycle that is fairly predictable in the time-span that it lasts. However, for an organization without the inevitablility of a death, lifespans can be indefinite. On the other hand, transitioning between stages of the lifecycle, while sometimes difficult for biological forms, can be potentially fatal for organizations, as we shall see later on. These differences notwithstanding, the lifecycle analogy is a useful way of thinking about and analyzing organizations, particularly in regards to the different leadership needs the organization has through its different lifestages.

If we look at an organization's lifecycle, shown in Figure 1.1, we can see that it can be divided into five distinct phases: Creation, Growth, Maturity, Turnaround, and Decline. Just as humans have different priorities and goals at different phases of their lifecycle, so organizations have different strategic priorities and goals throughout the organizational lifecycle.

Creation

The creation phase is the early entrepreneurial stage of the company as the entrepreneur assembles the beginnings of an organization geared towards bringing the organization's first product or service to market. The strategic priority of the organization at this stage is speed to market. This phase is characterized by chaotic, frenzied action as the entrepreneur gathers people around a central vision for the organization. There is an urgency in the company's actions, which are geared towards getting the first product or service out of the door, to bring the lifeblood of revenue into the organization. The organization at this point is very flexible, with little bureaucracy or even systems and routines in place. There are usually relatively few people involved in the organization, such that the entrepreneur has an individual relationship and direct communication with each member of the organization. Much of the activity often revolves around problem-solving as each situation and set-back the organization is faced with may potentially be life threatening, and the entrepreneur and his or her team struggle to solve these problems as rapidly as possible.

Once the initial product or service has entered the marketplace and begins to be adopted by the market in an increasingly rapid manner, the organization enters a phase of exponential growth that is the next phase of its lifecycle.

Growth

When an organization's product receives rapid acceptance in the market-place, the growth rate of the organization itself can be phenomenal. Rapid growth, while certainly the desire of the company and its entrepreneurial founder, can stretch and strain the capacities of the organization. The organization needs to move swiftly from the initial chaotic, frenetic and responsive mode of activity to quickly deploy structure, systems and routines in order to cope with the rapid growth of the organization. While the strategic priority of this stage is clearly growth, this growth must be managed and accompanied by the discipline and structure needed to facilitate it without destroying the company through over- or under-investment. Cash flow can become a serious problem to organizations in this stage. If not managed properly, it can kill or seriously impede even companies that are making a paper profit.

While companies seek to sustain this period of rapid growth, eventually the growth rate of the organization will necessarily taper off as it becomes increasingly difficult to maintain the same rate of growth from a larger base. Thus companies transition from this period of rapid growth to a period of slower growth or maintaining their market position.

Maturity

When the company hits maturity and a period of stability in its market, the strategic priority takes a subtle shift from growth to market share. Growth is usually thought of as a within-company comparison – how much the company grows relative to its own size in the previous period.

A shift to a focus on market share recognizes that the high internal growth rates of the past are over, often due to reaching a dominant position in the market, or a maturing market. With this point of internal stability reached, there is a shift in focus to external competitors and how the company performs against these rather than against its prior self. The focus is now on maintaining and increasing the company's share of the maturing market and achieving market dominance. This phase of the lifecycle can and, in most successful companies, does last the longest period of time, and can be sustained indefinitely. Thus, most of the large, established "blue-chip" businesses are within this phase of the lifecycle. Hence, you see companies such as General Electric focused on being the number one or number two player in each market it is in – a clear reflection of its focus on market share. Similarly, it is why analysts who follow a company such as Coca-Cola focus on volume growth, unit case sales, and tenths of a point of market share as better indicators of company progress than quarter-by-quarter profits, as these measures better show how the company is faring in terms of market share.

After a sustained period of maturity, companies may slip into a period of decline and need a turnaround to regain their former position. Such a slip in performance can either be caused externally, such as the market for the companies' products disappearing or declining because of market discontinuities or substitute products coming to the fore, or can be caused internally by organizational hubris. Danny Miller, in *The Icarus Paradox*,[10] describes how exceptionally successful companies bring about their own downfall by the overpursuit of their own competences to the extent that they become their own major fault and blindspot. Organizational hubris ensues when companies fail to recognize that they have more to learn and need to respond to changing market conditions. When this occurs, organizational performance will eventually begin to slip and a turnaround is needed for the organization to regain its past performance, or even to survive.

Turnaround

The key factor for an organization in decline is to realize that it is in fact in decline. It is often easy for companies to pass off incremental declines in revenue or market share to cyclical downturns or external circumstances which will soon right themselves, without recognizing the fundamental shift in the direction of the company. Marshall Meyer and Lynne Zucker, in their book *Permanently Failing Organizations*,[11] detail how large firms can slip into this state of permanent decline, slowly slipping in market share and revenues, selling off assets as needed to fund continuing operations, waiting for cyclical upturns to temporarily boost revenues and profits without ever addressing the underlying problems of the organization.

If, however, the company is able to recognize the fundamental shift in its performance in the marketplace, then the strategic priority can shift to one of reversing the decline of the organization, whether this be in market share of their existing market or, if their decline parallels a decline in their overall market, by seeking out and developing new markets. Often this leads to turmoil within the organization as routines have to be unlearned, structures reconfigured and strategies redirected. The power structure in the organization can also shift substantially, leading to great resistance from those who benefited from the old power structure. All this implies that chaos can and, to a certain extent, needs to return to the organization as it refocuses its vision on a new direction.

If the company fails to effect a turnaround, or after successive turn-around attempts falls into further decline, the organization moves into the final stage in its lifecycle.

Decline

Once the organization is in terminal decline, such that it is not viable as an independent entity, the strategic focus switches to realizing value. Organizations do not have to be headed inexorably towards bankruptcy to be in terminal decline, but can reach this point because of many other factors, such as being unable to reach or maintain an optimally efficient scale. Jag Sheth and Rajendra Sisodia have observed that industries are consolidating worldwide to obey what they term *The Rule of Three*;[12] that there can only be three major competitors in any given market. In industry after industry, Sheth and Sisodia describe how the industry has consolidated around three major players, with other players either going out of business, withdrawing to small niche markets, or being acquired by one of the three major players. Thus being acquired by a larger firm is one way an organization can realize value for its shareholders even though it is in terminal decline. Merging with similar sized firms to achieve scale, breaking the company up and selling assets or profitable divisions are other options for achieving value whilst in terminal decline.

Leadership Lifecycle

Through the description of firms at different stages of the organization's lifecycle, it should be clear that there are unique challenges facing organizations at each of the different stages. Consequently, it should be no surprise that it takes very different managerial and leadership skills to lead an organization at these different stages. Hence the Leadership Lifecycle. While there has been a long search for the characteristics that make a great leader, it is evident from these vastly different challenges that organizations face over the course of the lifecycle that there is no one perfect leadership style or set of leadership characteristics which are universally applicable across all situations. However, all is not lost. By studying and applying the lifecycle of organizations, it also becomes clear that the leadership task, and hence the leadership qualities required, vary systematically enough across organizations within the lifecycle to provide a useful guide to assessing the appropriate leadership qualities needed for a particular organization at a particular time.

While the next few chapters go into greater detail on the leadership characteristics needed at each stage of the lifecycle, let me briefly introduce the different leadership roles here that parallel the stages of the organization's lifecycle.

The Creator

As the label implies, the Creator role is to create the organization from scratch. The Creator breathes life into the organization, and provides that creative spark of energy to establish the organization out of nothing. The drive behind the Creator's spirit is his or her sense of vision for the organization, which lays out the heroic mission that is the organization's *raison d'être*. This vision is accompanied by an intense passion for the mission that energizes those around the Creator. It is this energy and focused passion that enable the Creator to instill the sense of urgency in the organization which is needed to focus on the organization's strategic priority of getting the product or service to market. The Creator needs to be comfortable dealing in an environment with little structure, where rapid change is a routine part of the prevailing environment. The Creator needs to be able to adapt constantly to this turbulence, while maintaining focus on the end goal of speed to market for the organization's product or service.

The Accelerator

In the period of rapid growth for the organization, the Accelerator needs to "put the pedal to the metal" for the organization to accelerate along an exponential growth path. The leadership role here is very different from that of the Creator. While the role of the Creator is essentially birthing the organization and providing an overarching vision for the organization, the Accelerator translates the heroic mission set by the Creator into systems and routines to enable the organization to grow without bursting at the seams. At this point in the lifecycle, the organization is rapidly changing internally to keep pace with its growth, but also needs to have more of an external focus on the market as the organization seeks to grow market share and dominate its niche. Thus, the Accelerator requires a high degree of focus and direction, and needs to be adept at communicating both internally and externally to the organization using a variety of media, and to be able to balance the internal needs of the organization for the details of robust systems, with external needs to communicate to and understand the needs of the organization's market, and often, financial markets.

The Sustainer

When the organization moves from a rapid growth stage to a more steady state of maturity, the leadership qualities needed in the organization also change. Not only are the leadership qualities of an exemplary Creator or Accelerator not applicable to an organization in maturity, but they can even be destructive. Indeed, many organizations have a very difficult time moving from the Creator entrepreneur, or the driving Accelerator, to finding the right leadership for a more mature stage, and we consequently see organizations go into rapid decline due to a failure to make this transition successfully. While the organization is in rapid growth mode, flexibility and change are paramount, and a chaotic culture can be advantageous rather than a drawback. However, as the company matures, structure and predictability become more necessary and consistency overtakes flexibility as the more essential quality. The emphasis moves from thriving in a chaotic environment at a frantic pace, to reducing chaos and steadying the pace. Therefore leading in this mature environment is a very different task to leading in the growth phase. Rather than the task of creating a vision faced by the Creator and translating that vision into reality that is faced by the Accelerator, the Sustainer needs to be able to initiate only incremental change, and reiterate and refine the mission. While this task seems simpler than the prior tasks of the Creator and Accelerator, the challenge lies in maintaining the enthusiasm of the organization to keep focus on an unchanging mission for a prolonged period of time.

The characteristics of direction, focus, passion, and communication skills still apply to the Sustainer, but their emphasis is different. The Accelerator's task of direction-setting and focus is in breaking down the intangible vision into tangible steps to bring the vision into reality, and in scaling systems in a time of rapid growth. In contrast, reality already exists when the Sustainer takes the helm. The Sustainer's role is to constantly seek improvements in efficiency, refining the organization's tasks so that they run ever more smoothly, and to transpose today's reality into a refined future state. The passion that needs to be shown by the Sustainer is not the "caution to the winds" variety often portrayed by the Creator and used to attract people to the organization's mission, but an unbridled enthusiasm, which serves to encourage the troops in the trenches of the organization. The nature of communication and the communication skills required of the leader also change. As the organization matures, the emphasis of communication needed from the leader shifts from an internal focus to a more external focus. While the organization is being built, the most vital communication is to those who will transform the vision into reality – the employees. When the organization matures, while internal communication is still important, the external constituencies take up an increasing amount of the leader's time, and so the Sustainer needs to be able to communicate effectively with analysts, the media, and other external groups to a larger degree than does the Creator or even the Accelerator, as the outside world plays a more important part in the leadership role.

The Transformer

When the organization is no longer able to sustain success and falls into decline, yet another set of leadership skills is required, that of the Transformer. In some respects the Transformer has a similar role to that of the Creator, except that the task is re-creation from an existing and declining base, rather than starting from scratch. This poses different challenges for the Transformer than those facing the Creator. The Transformer's first major task is to halt the decline of the organization. This entails changing the processes and direction of the organization and redefining the mission. Overcoming resistance to change within the organization is the biggest obstacle to renewal, and this fact can make the task of transforming an organization harder than that of creating it originally, as old ways and processes have to be dismantled and unlearned before a new vision can be established.

The Transformer, as re-creator, needs skills similar to those possessed by the Creator. However, whereas the Creator needs to implant a new heroic mission into empty space and make that vision a reality, the Transformer needs to put the newly defined vision in the context of a transformation of the old mission and overcome the failures of the past. While this can seem the more intractable task, the fact that the organization is in crisis and may be fighting for its very survival can be a benefit for the Transformer, as the stark threat of extinction can provide enough impetus for change to overcome the inertial forces of the status quo.

The Terminator

While an organization in decline will usually seek a Transformer to reignite the vision for the organization and turn around its ailing performance, there are occasions when the organization comes to a natural end, or where the strategic desire of the owners is to be acquired. This is a very different leadership role from any of the four previous roles, as the leader seeks to guide the ending of the organization, at least in its state of independence, rather than grow it or restore it to health. The timeframe of the organization switches from long-term horizons to short-term objectives. The strategic orientation goes from growth or position maintenance to value realization. Whether the organization is being wound down, or is shopping around for a buyer, the paramount leadership challenge is in addressing the uncertainties of what lies ahead, and overcoming employees' fears for the future. A major challenge is in retaining the focus of employees essential to the winding down or selling of the organization, when the temptation for many is to jump ship at the earliest opportunity.

Transitions within the Leadership Lifecycle

Even from these brief descriptions, it is apparent that just as the organization changes significantly from phase to phase in its lifecycle, so the corresponding leadership role also changes dramatically. It should be no surprise then that the transition from one phase to the next can be traumatic for the organization. Not only does the strategic orientation of the organization shift, but the necessary leadership characteristics, skills, and behaviors also change. These points, as shown in Figure 1.2, represent not

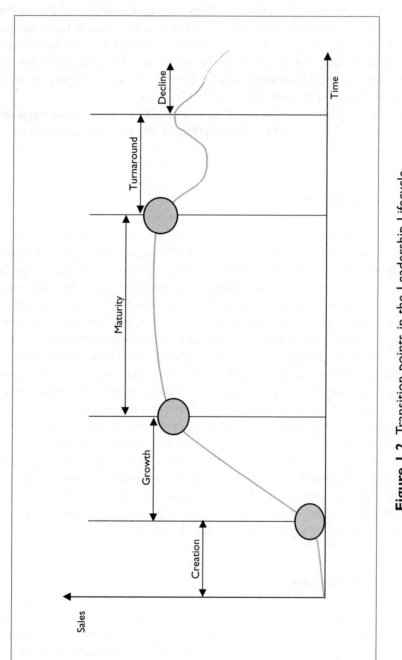

Figure 1.2 Transition points in the Leadership Lifecycle

only transition points, but also danger points for the organization and the leader. It is at these points that we often see organizations fail due to the inability to successfully make the transition, and it is also at these danger points where we observe forced departures of leaders who have been successful at the prior phase of the organization's lifecycle, but who are unable or unwilling to change their leadership role to the requirements of the organization in the next phase of its lifecycle.

Although Chapter 7 will extend the discussion of transitions through the Leadership Lifecycle, a brief description of the major danger points is appropriate here.

Creation to Growth

When the skills of the Creator coincide with a favorable external environment, a successful organization is born. As the organization goes through a period of rapid growth, the chaotic creative skills of the Creator flourish, but only up to a certain point. When the organization grows beyond a size where the Creator can have his or her hand directly in every part of the organization, a different form of leadership is required. Many entrepreneurial Creators have a hard time letting go of the organization they have built and either struggle to keep it at a point at which they can still control it, or desperately try to go beyond their capacity to manage, and the organization spins out of control. Ironically, the heroic mission, so important for the founding of the organization, can become its death sentence, as the Creator cannot pass on the baton to someone else before the vision has been accomplished in the eyes of the Creator. Unfortunately, this is not an uncommon event. Many organizations that were successful under their Creator founder fail to make the transition to a leader who can take on the role of the Accelerator, and consequently go into rapid decline. The opening examples above of govWorks and BigWords.com are prime examples of the failure to make this first transition.

Growth to Maturity

As growth tapers off, or the market in which the organization operates matures, the tendency – and character – of the hard-charging Accelerator is to try and maintain a very aggressive growth rate, beyond that which the market or organization can bear. This can cause the organization to hit a wall as the Accelerator overinvests in the infrastructure and inventory required for rapid growth, when the potential for continued growth has disappeared, damaging the financial health of the organization, and potentially putting it in jeopardy. This rise to maturity is also often a period of intense frustration for the growth-oriented Accelerator whose role and desire have been to rapidly expand the organization. Consequently, as the frustration level rises for the Accelerator and he or she becomes less successful in achieving the desired growth, this is another point at which we often see a change in leadership of the organization to a person more suited to the Sustainer role.

Maturity to Decline

In a company that has achieved lasting success over a sustained period, it is hard to avoid some complacency creeping into the organization. At the extreme, it develops into Danny Miller's Icarus paradox, mentioned previously, when the very characteristics that made the organization successful can, like the mythological Icarus's ascent towards the sun, lead to their downfall. Even in less extreme cases, a slow descent can be preceded by a lack of awareness of the changes taking place around the organization and how the requirements for success in the marketplace have changed, often relying on the ill-fated assumption that what has made the organization successful in the past will continue to make it successful going forward. The cause of this downfall is usually due to the organization's hubris, or what I term the "heroic self-concept." The heroic self-concept of a corporation can permeate the entire organization and cause its decline, as it becomes more insular and cut off from the realities of a changing environment. Also, because the psychological nature of heroic self-concept becomes pervasive within the organization, and especially at the top (indeed, this is where it is likely to start), it is rare that a leader who has succumbed to heroic self-concept, both personally and organizationally, will be able to lead the required organizational renewal. Thus the transition from the role of Sustainer to Transformer normally requires new leadership, and most frequently this new leadership has to come from outside the organization, as those people within the organization who could step into a leadership position from an organizational standpoint are usually also suffering from the same condition.

It is important to emphasize that the leadership roles of Creator, Accelerator, Sustainer, Transformer, and Terminator are roles and not individuals. This has two implications. First, the characteristics required for each of the different roles are not necessarily contained in any given individual.

So, for example, not every entrepreneur starting an organization will embody all the characteristics given here for a Creator. Nevertheless, the entrepreneur is seeking to fill the creative role and the characteristics of the Creator are generally needed in this role. Thus, some entrepreneurs may recognize where they are lacking specific leadership characteristics of the Creator role and supplement them through supporting roles played by others in the organization.

The second implication is that some individuals may exemplify more than one role and therefore have the ability to make the transition from one leadership role to another, either within the same organization, or across multiple organizations. It is also true that these leadership roles embodied in one individual may not be sequential in the Leadership Lifecycle. One of the examples which we will explore in more depth later is Steve Jobs of Apple Computer, who initially played the role of the entrepreneurial Creator of Apple, and having left the company, returned successfully as a Transformer when the company was suffering a decline.

Having outlined the construct of the Leadership Lifecycle, the rest of the book will examine each of the roles in more depth. Chapters 2 to 6 will examine the leadership roles of Creator, Accelerator, Sustainer, Transformer, and Terminator, respectively. Chapter 7 will highlight the transition or danger points between the successive phases of the lifecycle. Chapter 8 will give examples of leaders who are able to span roles across the Leadership Lifecycle. Chapters 9 and 10 will provide two in-depth case studies of The Walt Disney Company and British retail icon Marks & Spencer, as they go through their lifecycles. Finally, in Chapter 11, I examine what the Leadership Lifecycle implies for leaders, aspiring leaders and those who appoint leaders and are responsible for developing leadership at all levels in organizations across the lifecycle.

Notes

1. Hegedus, Chris, and Noujaim, Jehane. 2001. *Startup.com*. Pennebaker Hegedus Films and Noujaim Films.
2. Bayers, Chip. 2001. Crash course. *Wired*, March, pp. 92–102.
3. Bennets, L. 1979. Many widows find a new life running husband's business. *The New York Times*, September 24.
4. Cribbin, James, J. 1981. *Leadership: Strategies for Organizational Effectiveness*. New York: Amacom, p. 48.
5. de Geus, Arie. 1997. *The Living Company: Habits for Survival in a Turbulent Business Environment*. Boston, MA: Harvard Business School Press.
6. Kristof, Kathy M. 2002. Personal, Business Bankruptcy Filings Soar. *Los Angeles Times*, February 20, Business Section, p. 4.

7. Levinson, Daniel J., with Darrow, Charlotte N., Klein, Edward B., Levinson, Maria H., and McKee, Braxton. 1978. *The Season's of a Man's Life*. New York: Ballantine Books.

8. Chapman, S.J., and Ashton, T.S. 1914. The sizes of businesses, mainly in the textile industry. *Journal of the Royal Statistical Society*, Vol. 77. pp. 510–22, p. 512.

9. Kimberly, John R., Miles, Robert H., and associates. 1980. *The Organizational Lifecycle: Issues in the Creation, Transformation, and Decline of Organizations*. San Francisco: Jossey-Bass.

10. Miller, Danny. 1990. *The Icarus Paradox: How Exceptional Companies Bring about Their Own Downfall*. New York: HarperBusiness.

11. Meyer, Marshall W., and Zucker, Lynne G. 1989. *Permanently Failing Organizations*. Newbury Park, CA: Sage.

12. Sheth, Jagdish, and Sisodia, Rajendra. 2002. *The Rule of Three: Why Only Three Major Competitors will Survive in any Market*. New York: Free Press.

CHAPTER 2

The Creator

Organizations are founded by visionary Creators. The Creator develops or embodies an idea that is too great to be accomplished by a single individual, necessitating the formation of an organization to bring it to fruition. The energy and passion that the Creator has for the idea attract others, stimulating them to follow the Creator in his or her entrepreneurial venture. Behind this idea, the entrepreneurial Creator is usually driven by a quest for immortality – seeking to make a contribution that will not be readily eroded by the sands of time. In his book on CEO retirement, *The Hero's Farewell*,[1] Yale University's Jeffrey Sonnenfeld identified the concept of heroic mission as an internal feeling that one (the leader or hero) has a unique role to fill and that only the hero is capable of carrying out the responsibilities of the job. This concept is captured by the nineteenth-century social reformer John Ruskin, in his statement "Really great men have a curious feeling that the greatness is not in them but through them." This feeling that their existence should make a difference to the world in which they live is the strongest common characteristic among successful Creators. It is, however, also the characteristic that ultimately leads to the failure of many of the organizations they create, as the Creator fails to let the organization progress into the next stage of its lifecycle.

The heroic mission is developed in the Creator, and is strengthened over time to the point where it becomes a coherent objective, or mission, in which the hero sees him or herself as the focal point for change in the world. This is not necessarily a dramatic world-shaking event, although often the hero's mission is described and encapsulated in grandiose terms – terms that describe the effect of the change on people's lives, rather than the innovation or change per se. The Creator creates the organization in order to accomplish the heroic mission, as the achievement of this vision is beyond the capacities of a single individual.

Steve Jobs, founder of Apple Computer, is driven by this very belief that he can make a significant difference to the lives of others, and cumulatively to society as a whole, and that in so doing is making a significant contribution to history. After the success of Apple's initial product, the Apple II computer, Jobs visited a school where the computers were being used in the classroom:[2]

> I felt it the first time when I visited a school. It had 3rd and 4th graders in a classroom one time and they had a whole classroom full of Apple II's. And I spent a few hours there, and I saw these 3rd and 4th graders growing up completely different than I grew up because of this machine. And what hit me about it was here was this machine that a very few people designed. About four in the case of the Apple II. And they gave it to some people who didn't know how to design it but they knew how to make it, to manufacture it, and they could make a whole bunch of them. They gave it to some people who didn't know how to design or manufacture it but they knew how to distribute it. And they gave it to some people who didn't know how to design it or manufacture it or distribute it, but they knew how to write software for it. And gradually this sort of inverse pyramid grew and when it finally got into the hands of a lot of people it blossomed out of this tiny little seed. And it seemed like an incredible amount of leverage and it all started with just an idea. And here was this idea taken through all of these stages resulting in a classroom full of kids growing up with some insights and some fundamentally different experiences which I thought might be very beneficial to their lives because of this germ of an idea a few years ago.

> And that's an incredible feeling to know that you had something to do with it and to know it can be done. To know that you can plant something in the world and it will grow. And change the world ever so slightly.

What makes Creator leaders stand out, apart from their sense of heroic mission, is their continued passion for this vision, normally so intense that it pervades the atmosphere around them – no-one who comes into contact with them has any doubt as to their purpose. Their unbounded energy and devotion to their mission draw others to them and consequently to embrace the vision of the leader. Two mold-breaking Creators from the retail industry, Anita Roddick of The Body Shop and Sam Walton of Wal-Mart, provide excellent examples of how passionate commitment is essential in a successful Creator.

Anita Roddick, The Body Shop

Anita Roddick founded The Body Shop in 1976 in order to "make profits with principles." Like most successful Creators, Anita exudes energy and passion, and embodies the mission of the organization that she founded. Against all odds, Anita succeeded in taking a single store in Brighton, England, to a chain of over 1,900 stores across 50 countries crossing 12 time zones. In describing the phenomena of The Body Shop and how her energy and passion played an important part in making The Body Shop a reality, she states that "to succeed, you have to believe in something with such a passion that it becomes a reality,"[3] and believes that "a fundamental shortcoming in much of business today is that the leadership lacks vision and passion – the two most important ingredients to inspire and motivate."[4] She continues on:

> In The Body Shop we have both in abundance and we possess, in addition, a further secret ingredient: an extraordinary level of optimism, almost amounting to euphoria, which permeates the whole company. We are incurable optimists – and incurable optimists believe they can do anything.[5]

> You educate people, especially young people, by stirring their passions. So you take every opportunity to grab the imagination of your employees, you get them to feel they are doing something important, that they are not a lone voice, that they are the most powerful and potent people on the planet. It is finding a way of bonding with the company and producing a sense of passion that you would never find in Selfridge's or Bloomingdale's.[6]

> How do you ennoble the spirit when you are selling something as inconsequential as a cosmetic cream? You do it by creating a sense of holism, of spiritual development, of feeling connected to the workplace, the environment and relationships with one another. It's how to make Monday to Friday a sense of being alive rather than slow death. How do you give people a chance to do a good job? By making them feel good about what they are doing. The spirit soars when you are satisfying your own basic material needs in such a way that you are also serving the needs of others honorably and humanely. Under these circumstances, I can even feel great about a moisturizer.[7]

> As to our passion, no one – not even our most cynical critics – can deny that we are passionate in everything we say and do: The Body Shop positively radiates passion. I can't bear to be around people who are bland or bored or uninterested (or to employ them). The kind of brain-dead, gum-chewing assistants you find in so many shops drive me wild. I want everyone who works for us to feel the

same excitement that I feel; to share my passion for education and customer care and communication and motivation and to put it into practice. [8]

Here we see both Anita's sense of passion, her sense of heroic mission, and how it pervades the enterprise providing an optimism that believes it can overcome every obstacle. This passionate belief in what they are doing allows even a business which sells everyday, mundane products, such as cosmetics, to have a mission that is portrayed by the Creator as having societal importance.

Sam Walton, Wal-Mart

It is tempting to think of passion as a nicety – something that adds to a Creator's ability to rally the troops and get people fired up, but is not really essential for an effective organization in the Creation phase. However, this mode of reasoning is refuted by Sam Walton, the entrepreneurial founder of the world's largest retailer, Wal-Mart. In his autobiography, *Made in America*, he recounts "Sam's 10 Rules for Building a Business." Right at the very top of the list, rule number one reads:[9]

> Commit to your business. Believe in it more than anybody else. I think I over-came every single one of my personal shortcomings by the sheer passion I brought to my work. I don't know if you're born with this kind of passion, or if you can learn it. But I do know that you need it. If you love your work, you'll be out there every day trying to do the best you possibly can, and pretty soon everybody around will catch the passion from you – like a fever.

You can't get a more emphatic confirmation than that about the centrality of passion to the Creator's leadership role. In order to gain the commitment of others to the Creator's vision, the Creator himself must be passionately committed to it – and that passion must come through every day through the leader's own enthusiasm for the task. In the case of Sam Walton, this included Saturday morning meetings with all his managers at 7am beginning with a rousing Arkansas Razorbacks cheer – meetings that he had been preparing for at 3 or 4am that morning, studying the figures for each store. It included doing the outrageous – betting his team that they could not exceed a performance target, and then following through with the payment of that bet, whether it was performing the hula on Wall Street or kissing a pig.

Creators are comfortable in taking risks, but do their best to calculate and minimize those risks. When they take risks, it is in the pursuit of their vision. Also, what outsiders may see as risks may not be perceived as risks by the Creators themselves. Instead the Creators see these decisions and actions as merely essential steps in the pursuit of their vision. Returning to the example of Steve Jobs at Apple Computer, this time in the creation of the Macintosh, Jobs spoke of the pursuit of the vision over the risks of Macintosh failing in the market:

> You have to make a lot of decisions based on the fragrance or odor of where you think things are going. We think the Mac will sell zillions, but we didn't build the Mac for anybody else. We built it for ourselves. We were the group of people who were going to judge whether it was great or not.[10]

Here, Jobs is saying that it is the vision for the product that was important to them, not whether or not the marketplace accepted it. Thus, they would be the ones who determined whether the vision had been achieved rather than through external validation. This, of course, takes the pursuit of the vision to the extreme, but it does demonstrate the centrality of the vision to the Creator. Indeed, the focus on the vision of a perfect personal computer has been a double-edged sword for Apple. While it has certainly produced breakthrough computers in terms of design and ease of use in line with the vision, the lack of attention to the demands of the marketplace, and the unwillingness to allow their designs to be adulterated by third-party add-ons has led to some spectacular product failures, and the company as a whole being relegated to a small niche in the overall PC market.

The Creator's Task

The Creator's first task is in selling the vision for the organization. The Creator's passion for the vision is key in enabling him or her to generate enthusiasm for the idea from the first key people who form the core team of the organization and, in most cases, also in searching for capital from outside sources such as venture capitalists or angel investors. Often the Creator's task of selling the vision for the organization to these two constituents of a core team and potential investors is necessarily simultaneous as investors may be reluctant to invest without the identification of a core team that the investors are confident can bring the vision to reality, and the team members may not be able to commit to the fledgling organization until funding is in place. This often makes for a tricky balance for the Creator, trying to get commitment from his or her core team to form the organization around the vision without the certainty of funding in place. However, this also has the positive effect of screening out the type of people who are not comfortable in the uncertain and chaotic environment of an organization in the Creation phase, and gaining the commitment of those who are fully engaged in the vision of the organization.

Once the core team is in place, the task of the Creator switches to one of breaking down the vision into practical steps to get the product or service developed and into the marketplace as quickly as possible. It is not enough for a Creator to espouse a grand vision of what the organization is aiming for at some far off point in the future; the Creator must be able to translate this heroic mission into actionable steps that can be accomplished in relatively short periods and are achievable by organization members, either individually or collectively.

This delineation of the vision into smaller, achievable steps also has the important effect of establishing credibility for the vision. A vision that is described in grand terms without the associated steps as to how it is to be accomplished is seen as unachievable and, consequently, lacks credibility. By extension, the Creator will also then lack credibility and will not attract followers, or those initially attracted will rapidly fall away, no matter how passionately the Creator is personally devoted to the vision. People will not pursue a Creator's vision unless they believe it is achievable. Thus the delineation of the vision into specific actionable steps is essential for the Creator to establish the vision as achievable and credible.

The flip side of breaking down the vision into small, achievable goals is that the Creator must maintain the context of the smaller goals within the larger vision. It is not sufficient to espouse solely the small goals in isolation; these often mundane tasks which need to be performed as early foundations for the mission are not easy to perceive as essential, and need to be put in the context of their impact on achieving the larger vision. Indeed, it is more important for the Creator to emphasize the essential nature of these mundane, routine and less obviously vital tasks than it is to elevate those tasks which are making visible progress along the path to achieving the mission, as these tasks have intrinsic psychic rewards built into them. While this sounds obvious, it is often the visible progress that is made and high-profile tasks that are undertaken that are more often celebrated within most organizations rather than the essential, but more mundane deeds which are still necessary to achieve the organization's vision.

A useful analogy that describes the role of the Creator in breaking the vision into small component parts while maintaining the focus on the overarching vision is of a person who needs bifocal spectacles. With only long distance lenses, the things far away are perfectly in focus, but things close at hand are a blur. Similarly, with only reading glasses, things immediately close are focused, but those further away are blurred. The person needs bifocals in order to be able to switch back and forth between things that are near and things that are far off – to put the close details in the perspective of the larger picture. Even so, it is difficult to see both clearly at once, and the person needs to become comfortable flitting back and forth almost unconsciously between the two perspectives to be able to use the bifocals effectively. At first, flitting back and forth takes conscious effort, and can be a strain on the eyes, but it soon becomes second nature. The task of the Creator is to provide the bifocal lenses to the organization – to provide and clarify the long-term vision and also to provide a focus on the short-term details, and to relate those details to the distant vision. The Creator then needs to become comfortable, and make others in the organization comfortable, in continually switching back and forth between the short- and long-term goals, relating one to the other.

A related task for the Creator is to develop an organizational ability to focus on many different details simultaneously. Whereas what we have just looked at concerned the vertical connection between long- and short-term goals – how a specific short-term goal fits into the long-term vision – this aspect has to do with the horizontal focus – looking at many different short-terms goals at one time.

To focus on one aspect of the vision to the exclusion of other aspects leads to an excess of that one thing and a deprivation in others, which, like any food to a human, is disastrous. A human needs a balanced diet, and will become ill if he or she eats one thing exclusively, even though that one food may be good and necessary for good health when balanced with the other elements of a healthy diet. Similarly, in a business context, a balanced 'diet' of focus is required – a single focus on any one aspect of the business, whether it is human resources, financial control, going the extra mile for the customer, or any other aspect, while a vital ingredient of a complete strategy, can prove disastrous if followed exclusively to the detriment of other essential elements. David Glass, successor to Sam Walton as chairman and CEO of Wal-Mart, the world's largest and most successful retail chain, said of founder Sam Walton:

> One thing you'll notice if you spend very much time talking with Sam about Wal-Mart's success. He's always saying things like "This is the key to the whole thing," or "That was our real secret." He knows as well as anyone that there wasn't any magic formula. A lot of different things made it work, and in one day's time he may cite all of them as the "key" or the "secret." What's amazing is that for almost fifty years he's managed to focus on all of them at once – all the time. That's his real secret.[11]

I would contend that the lack of horizontal focus is one of the biggest causes of failure in large and small businesses, and especially in young businesses in the Creation stage where their typical small size makes them more vulnerable to mistakes of this nature. The biggest single cause of failure among small businesses is not lack of profitability or the inability to serve the customer or not having the right product or the lack of good marketing ability – a surprising number of small businesses have all these elements and yet fail through lack of cash flow. They grow too fast, concentrate on selling, producing and serving the customer, and pay little attention to actually getting the money in the bank and planning adequately for growth. Consequently, their early success in the market kills them because they don't have the cash flow to survive in the short term. In other words, they fail to make the transition from the Creation to Growth phases of the lifecycle. Being the best in any area is not enough if the broad focus across all the necessary elements for survival is not there. For these young businesses, and indeed every business, the maxim should be: if you don't survive in the short term, there is no long term.

The Creator's Organization

The Creator's domain is the Creation phase of the organizational lifecycle. This phase spans from the beginning of the evolving vision for an organization in the Creator's mind, to the initial launch of the product or service into the marketplace and early adoption of that product by the market. During this phase, the organization itself is in a constant state of rapid change, and may be almost unrecognizable from the state of the organization at the beginning of this phase to its state at the end. However, the strategic focus and the vision of the organization remain the same throughout the phase, with the priority being speed to market – getting the product or service introduced into the market as quickly as possible.

In the very beginning of the Creation phase, the organization may not even be recognizable as an organization, with just a few people gathered around pursuing the Creator's vision. The organization is probably in search of capital and fleshing out the vision into a saleable business plan, and the activity in the organization, although frenetic, is pursuing multiple directions. At this point there are few if any procedures in place for anything; decisions are made as issues arise, people are hired as needed and that hiring is based more on their enthusiasm and perceived fit with the evolving personality of the organization rather than detailed screening of applicants' skills and qualifications.

People who are attracted to companies at this very early Creation phase tend also to be very entrepreneurial, are willing to dedicate themselves to the mission put forth by the Creator, and comfortable with the lack of structure and chaotic activity. These early evangelists for the organization are fully engaged in trying to realize the vision and will act in entrepreneurial ways to make sure that vision is realized. This was true in the early days of ESPN, the sports television network. Stephen Anderson, one of the early employees and later director of production, described the early beginnings of the network as characterized by a workforce of youthful upstarts:

> Young, young people who were just happy to be getting a shot in the business. The work ethic was defined by endless hours of labor put in by people who were just thrilled to be here. It was everywhere you turned in the company. We were understaffed almost every place you looked, with people performing two or three jobs, working day after day with no days off. Most people were not married. Nobody seemed to have kids at the time. People felt a real pride in the fact that they worked 20 days straight or were here all night long. The people were very young and did not have a whole lot else to concern themselves with except for their careers.[12]

Similar to most companies in the Creation phase, the early days of ESPN were characterized by a spirit of individual initiative. One manager captured the last-minute sense of urgency in the organization by describing the typical ESPN employee as "the kind of person who did their home-work on the bus on the way to school." At ESPN, one telling incident of the entrepreneurial spirit that pervades the culture at Creation phase companies made the newspapers. At 3:40am one November night, a winter snowstorm knocked out ESPN's main broadcast generator at its Bristol, Connecticut production headquarters, and the back-up generator would not start. All ESPN transmissions ceased. Ralph Voigt, an ESPN engineer, was called and began the five-mile drive from his home in the Bristol hills. When he arrived at the station, he led an expedition of hearty technicians into the storm. They strung together several automobile jump leads, attaching one end to a small operating generator that provides power to ESPN's administrative offices and the other to the downed transmission generator. In so doing, they managed to jump-start the network. ESPN was back on the air at 7:31am.[13]

This entrepreneurial flexibility is characteristic of the Creation phase of organizations, and it is important to note that this responsiveness and adapt-ability to the challenges that come up for the organization are not only desir-able, but often essential for organizations in this phase. Often decisions are made without discussion or consensus-building. Experiments are made and, if successful, become part of the routines of the organization, and if not successful they are quickly discarded. Often it is the Creator who makes most of the decisions in this phase, although others may step in and take on entrepreneurial risks to keep the organization moving towards its vision, as we saw above with ESPN.

The Creator's Leadership Style

The Creator's personality has more of a dominating impact on the Creation phase than any of the other leadership roles in their respective phases, simply because the Creation organization is brand new without any prior culture beyond what is given to it by the Creator and the founding members of the organization. Because of the Creator's passionate vision for the organization, the culture that develops in the company is largely the shadow of the Creator's personality. The Creator usually dominates the decisions made by the organization, and is often seen as autocratic in style rather than participative, although this may simply be due to the fact that the vision is very much stronger and clearer in the mind of the Creator than in others. This can also make an autocratic style more effective in the early stages, as this can lead to a more direct decision path towards getting the product or service to market without diversions created by others with perhaps a more blurred view of the vision.

The strong personality of the Creator which comes to dominate the culture of the organization can lead to a charismatic attribution by the followers, seeing the Creator as an infallible or exceptional leader. Although now a widely used descriptor in the business vocabulary, the term "charisma" derives from the ancient Greek word *charismata*, meaning "gift," or more precisely, a "gift from the gods."[14] The term was later used by the Christian Church to describe spiritual gifts such as prophesy, healing, and divine wisdom. It was only relatively recently that the sociologist Max Weber in the first half of the twentieth century widened the use of the term to describe leaders, in his case, political leaders, who seemed to have a "charismatic gift" of supernatural or exceptional powers that set them apart from ordinary men. Weber's conceptualization of charisma had five principal components:

1. a person with extraordinary gifts

2. a crisis

3. a radical solution to the crisis

4. followers who are attracted to the exceptional person because they believe that they are linked through him or her to transcendent powers

5. validation of the person's gifts and transcendence in repeated experiences of success.[15]

We can see from these criteria why a Creator will often be considered charismatic. Expanding on the above list, we have a person starting up an organization with a vision for the future; repeated crises that become an everyday occurrence in a start-up business; reliance on the Creator for the solutions and decisions to overcome these crises and obstacles; the successful overcoming of obstacles facing the organization; and the opportunity for the followers to be a key part in bringing the vision to reality. This description of charisma provided by Weber also points to the Transformer as being potentially regarded as a charismatic leader due to the crisis nature of the obstacles facing the firm in decline, and indeed we often see Transformers hailed as charismatic. It also explains why we are less likely to see Accelerators and Sustainers heralded in the same way as Creators and Transformers, as their organizations are less prone to major crises.

Although Weber was retaining much of the original Greek and Christian meaning of the word "charisma," since that time its meaning has evolved further and is no longer seen as a gift bestowed by the Greek gods, and something inherent in the individual blessed with those gifts. Instead, charisma has come to be seen as something that is defined by others who are influenced by the leader's sense of vision and demonstrated passion for that mission. The Wharton School's Robert House and his colleagues, in their study of personality and charisma of U.S. presidents, redefined charisma as:

> a relationship or bond between the leader and subordinates or other followers, and although we do not define charisma as a personality trait of specific leaders, we argue that certain leader personality characteristics contribute to the formation of charismatic relationships with subordinates. Because charisma is a relationship and not a personality characteristic of leaders, charisma exists only if followers say it does or followers behave in a certain way.[16]

This charismatic relationship between the leader and his or her followers can have a large positive effect, inspiring followers who are dedicated to the vision of the leader, loyal to the leader and prepared to do whatever it takes to realize the vision. However, this relationship can also have its downsides. First, it can lead to a perception by followers of the infallibility of the leader. This is built up over time as the leader successfully navigates the organization through successive crises, and followers and the organization as a whole become increasingly dependent on the leader for all the decisions that need to be made. This can be dysfunctional in several ways. First, the leader is not infallible, and indeed the past success may lead to his or her own hubris and heroic self-concept, such that the leader takes increasingly risky and bad decisions believing in his or her own infallibility. Second, the charismatic relationship may blind followers so that they don't see the leader's increasing willingness to take risks and make bad decisions. Third, even if the leader continues to be successful, when the leader departs the organization it leaves such a void that the organization becomes fossilized into a state of constantly making decisions by trying to imagine what the departed leader would have done. We will see an example of this in Chapter 9 in the case study of The Walt Disney Company, which succumbed to this fossilization after the death of Walt Disney himself.

The other potentially dysfunctional aspect of charismatic relationships is that they often regress into a love/hate relationship between leader and follower as the expectations on both sides of the relationship continue to escalate over time. Jay Conger of the London Business School and the University of Southern California describes this love/hate relationship as akin to an addiction:

Many [charismatic leaders], though not all, seem to create love/hate feelings with their subordinates. They are tough and demanding, yet the reward of their praise is so confirming that subordinates describe it as an "emotional high" and, therefore, work hard for their leader's commendation. As a result, motivation and task accomplishment often exceed all expectations. But praise and rewards may soon become an addiction that, when denied, can make subordinates feel like outcasts.

Subordinates can become addicted to their leader's empowerment. The charismatic becomes a "quick fix" for feeling good about themselves. The trouble is that some subordinates have described this experience as an emotional rollercoaster. One minute they feel loved and respected; the next minute they feel unworthy. Clearly this dynamic creates an unhealthy dependency. As well, the charismatic empowers subordinates so they can achieve difficult tasks. But what if these tasks lead to disaster? Believing in their leader's faith and convictions, followers may simply escalate their commitment to tasks that are doomed.[17]

In so doing, the organization becomes very dependent on the leader and the talents and decision-making abilities of all others in the organization can tend to be wasted. Thus, while the charismatic relationship between the Creator and the followers in the Creator's organization can be immensely productive and helpful towards making the Creator's vision a reality, this relationship needs to be tempered and managed in order to successfully transition beyond the Creation phase of the organization's lifecycle.

Transition from Creation to Growth Phase

As the organization approaches the end of the Creation phase and the transition to the Growth stage, the needs of the organization begin to change. The organization has reached the point where its initial product or service has reached the marketplace and has experienced initial acceptance in the market. Orders are beginning to flow into the company. While this is what the organization has been working towards, it does not come without its own set of problems. As orders begin to come in, a routine begins to develop on how to handle them. Initial orders are dealt with on an ad hoc basis and individual attention is lavished on each order to ensure that the customer is satisfied. As the order flow increases, due to the lack of structure inherent in the Creation phase, difficulties can arise in filling orders in a timely manner, as flexibility rather than efficiency is the hallmark of the Creation phase organization. If order flow increases faster than systems are established, costs can spiral out of control, cash flow can tighten, and chaos can result in an increasing backlog of orders as the company struggles to cope with rising demand. Such difficulties, which push the limits of the informal structure and organization of the Creation phase company, indicate that the organization needs to move into the Growth phase and put more structured routines in place to cope with the growth that the organization is experiencing. Hence, as the organization moves from the Creation to Growth phase of the lifecycle, the focus of the leadership role required also switches from one of creating a vision to instituting systems and organization to allow the company to successfully grow. In other words, the main focus switches from the big picture of a grand future vision to a concern with the details of everyday processes in order to facilitate controlled growth.

Notes

1. Sonnenfeld, Jeffrey A. 1988. *The Hero's Farewell: What Happens when CEOs Retire.* New York: Oxford University Press.
2. From *Beyond Start Up* video program by Nathan & Tyler.
3. Roddick, Anita. 1991. *Body and Soul: Profits with Principles – The Amazing Success Story of Anita Roddick and The Body Shop.* New York: Crown. p. 86.
4. Ibid. pp. 225–6.
5. Ibid. p. 226.
6. Ibid. pp. 249–50.
7. Ibid. pp. 22–3.
8. Ibid. p. 218.
9. Walton, Sam, and Huey, John. 1992. *Sam Walton – Made in America: My Story.* New York: Doubleday. pp. 246–7.
10. Young, Jeffrey S. 1988. *Steve Jobs: The Journey is the Reward.* London: Glentop Press. p. 235.
11. See note 9, p. 245.
12. Interview with author.
13. *The New York Post*, November 21, 1986.
14. Conger, Jay. A. 1989. *The Charismatic Leader: Behind the Mystique of Exceptional Leadership.* San Francisco: Jossey-Bass.
15. Trice, H.M., and Beyer, J.M. 1986. Charisma and its routinization in two social movement organizations. *Research in Organizational Behavior*, Vol. 8: pp. 113–64.
16. House, R.J., Spangler, W.D., and Woycke, J. 1991. Personality and charisma in the U.S. Presidency: A psychological theory of leader effectiveness. *Administrative Science Quarterly*, **36**: 364–96. p. 366.
17. See note 13, p. 157.

CHAPTER 3

The Accelerator

Accelerators transform fledgling entrepreneurial businesses into powerful engines of growth. The Accelerator takes the entrepreneurial fledgling organization of the Creator and puts systems and structures in place to enable the organization to successfully grow and manage that growth. The Accelerator retains the same vision for the organization as the Creator but enables that vision to become a reality. The Accelerator is very much driven by detail, and attention to detail is far more important at this Growth phase of the lifecycle than in the Creation phase where the big picture vision was paramount. While the chaotic organization of the Creator provided necessary flexibility for the organization in the Creation phase, as the company establishes itself in the marketplace and gains acceptance, the Accelerator brings order to the chaos and focuses in on scalable routines, procedures, and systems to produce that order. As such, the primary focus moves from flexibility to efficiency as the strategic priority of the organization shifts from speed to market as the Creator attempts to get the product out of the door, to growth as the Accelerator seeks to accelerate growth in market share from the initial foothold that has been established.

By the time the Accelerator role comes to the forefront, the organization has reached the marketplace with its initial product or service offering. There is some semblance of an organization present, but there is often very little structure in place and decisions tend to be made on an ad hoc basis as problems arise. One prime example of an Accelerator is John Chambers, CEO of networking giant, Cisco Systems. A part of the folklore at Cisco is the story of how Chambers was late for his first board meeting when he took over as CEO because he took a call from a distressed customer and made certain that the problem was resolved before joining the meeting.[1] From this one incident at the beginning of his tenure, Chambers established the customer as the number one priority at Cisco and that decisions and systems revolved around satisfying the customer.

Instead of the Creator's singular focus of getting the product to market, the Accelerator has, on the one hand, to seek a balance between being flexible and open to change, not tied to the particular technology or product specification that the company is currently offering, while on the other, ensuring that innovations and changes to the product are immediately reliable for the customer in order to avoid damaging the organization's growing reputation. John Chambers is very conscious of the possibility of damaging the firm's reputation, yet is forthright about the way Cisco approaches this balance:

> We cannot, nor will we, do the same thing a start-up does, which is bring out a product and … not worry about customer satisfaction when you launch and let your customers shake it out for you. Our customers put our products straight into the core of the network that runs their business, and so the expectations of quality are high.[2]

> Cisco is kind of unique in that we have no religious technology. If a customer says this is what they're going to buy and we hear that from enough customers, that's what we build, regardless of what we think. We let the market determine it, and one of the unique advantages we bring is an architecture that allows our customers to pick and choose at given points and times which technology they want. I think companies who make the mistake of saying, "Here's where the industry's going," and "This is absolutely where you're going to be three to five years from now" are going to be very disappointed.[3]

The detail orientation of Chambers – the systems he has established, and the focus on the customer – is evident by his own behavior. Every evening, whether at home or on the road, Chambers personally checks on all Cisco's critical accounts, defined not by the dollar value of the account, but by how concerned the client, sales rep, or engineer is about a problem or the possibility of the client choosing someone else over Cisco. If an employee senses that an account is becoming critical, they are required to leave Chambers a voice mail on a special direct line, which Chambers checks daily. Chambers admits that "I'm probably the only CEO in the world in a company of this size who does this. But the fact that I pay attention to these issues at this level means that the whole company has to."[4] Chambers also does this to gain an early warning of potential competitive threats against the company or areas in which they are not satisfying the customer in some way. He notes, "If I get 13 or 15 reports of critical account activity, I know we've got serious problems. Real serious problems."[5]

The Accelerator's Organization

One of the major changes to the organization that often occurs under the governance of the Accelerator is for the company to go public and list its stock on a stock exchange. The transition to a public company brings a new set of problems in dealing with owners. Instead of vigilant and demanding venture capitalists, who often play an active role in monitoring their investment, the investment is now monitored by third parties, analysts on behalf of dispersed shareholders. The stock market can be every bit as demanding as the venture capitalists were, with ever increasing expectations, and a whole new set of rules and regulations to obey. The Accelerator needs to recognize the different needs of this new investment community and systematically devise a strategy of interpreting and relaying company information in a timely manner. Living in the public market places difficult demands on any company and moving from a private to a public company necessitates a considerable adjustment on the part of the company and can change the task or focus of the Accelerator. The presence of a large group of shareholders who are unfamiliar with the company's business forces the Accelerator to dedicate time and resources to communicating the organization's vision to this new audience. An infrastructure and procedures for dealing with investor education must be developed. Employees and even the Accelerator him- or herself must also be educated about the different challenges they will face as members of a public company. These challenges include creating an image that will appeal to investors, managing the image so that the stock price is stable, and courting investment analysts and institutional investors. In making this transition to a public company, the Accelerator's role has to include a much more external focus rather than concentrating solely on the internal operations of the organization.

Accelerators sometimes struggle to communicate their vision in a manner that appeals to the investment community. Many find it difficult to meet the expectations of an often short-sighted group of investors who demand improved financial results every quarter. The CEO of a company that sells large capital equipment to an international market discussed the effect of this problem on his company:

> The most difficult problem we have is that we are not a quarter-by-quarter business. The only way we're a quarter-by-quarter business is by our own

maturation and trying to shape ourselves to quarters. You look at the size of orders, I mean, typically we're dealing with $500,000 or $1,000,000 deals, so they're large orders compared to our revenue stream. You look also at the sales cycle when you're selling to Kazakhstan, I mean, they're politically involved and they're long cycles and somewhat unpredictable. So we have all that stuff to deal with, trying to shoehorn that into a corporate quarter is difficult.[6]

This change in status from a private to a public company not only has the danger of simply distracting the Accelerator from the more fundamental role of positioning the company for growth towards window-dressing for the outside investment community, but can also potentially lead to a more dangerous change of strategy to accommodate the perceived short-term orientation of investors. The CEO of a recently public small pharmaceutical company explained these pressures:

I'm generally not a complainer. I'm simply saying that it tends to bother me, and it tends to take a lot of energy from companies when you make the transition from development stage to mezzanine stage. You turn the corner on profitability, you become profitable, and immediately your company is perceived differently. The value of your company before you go public is basically based on intangibles, and even after you go public, when your company is still losing money, the valuation of your company is based on future value – so how do you quantify that? What is something worth? And the answer is, what someone will pay. But once you turn the corner into profitability, you have got to deal with the financial realities of life. And there is an ever-increasing need to do better than your last quarter. There is an emphasis on financial performance as opposed to long-term strategy, and it becomes distracting sometimes.

The problem in the United States today is that the public equity markets have very short-term horizons. That's why most investors, especially the people who invest in development stage health-care companies such as ours tend to have exit strategies in mind the minute they make the investment. And sometimes when you are trying to develop the product or a business area, or enhance the business in a certain area, you have a longer vision. So the romance with the company waxes and wanes more with quarterly reports than it does with the overall long-term strategy for the company. That troubles me sometimes.[7]

However, despite these complexities of being a public company, there is a large benefit which comes to organizations who take the plunge into the

public markets in the form of increased credibility and public awareness of
the organization, which can be enormously helpful to small, but fast-
growing companies in the Growth phase of the lifecycle. Bill O'Meara,
who, as CEO of the technology firm C-Cube Microsystems, took the
company public explained:

> Why did we go public? I think when you're calling on billion dollar customers,
> very, very big boy customers, the difference between being a privately owned
> company and a publicly held company is night and day. They see you differ-
> ently ... I think there was an important step that had to be taken from the stand-
> point of how our customers view us. Are we real? Are we going to be here two
> years from now? Are they prepared to commit major programs to this young,
> upstart company? So there was that benefit in the marketplace that we'd get by
> going public.[8]

The Accelerator's Task

As the organization moves from the Creation to Growth phase of the lifecycle, and particularly as it continues to move up the growth curve, the
attentions of the Accelerator, whether as a public or private company, shift
from an overwhelmingly internal focus on putting systems in place to
allow for growth, to a more external perspective on establishing key
relationships with customers, suppliers, and potential investors. The CEO
of an enterprise software company recognized the vital nature of personally building relationships with large customers who would prove vital in
establishing credibility and a track record for the company, in addition to
the revenue the accounts produced:

> I spend thirty, maybe forty percent of my time with end-user customers like
> Holiday Inn or Home Depot. A big piece of my time is talking to the customers
> about where we're going as a company vis-à-vis my other two competitors, so
> they've got a sense that we're here for the long-term making money in the
> business, and can stand competitive stress from anybody that might come into
> the business. Because the thing all of these customers don't want to have to do
> is change.[9]

As Cisco Systems grew such that the company moved from dealing
only with a relatively few large customers to a much broader array of
customers of different sizes, visibility became much more important to
Cisco. As well as beginning to advertise heavily in 2000 with its "Are you

ready?" campaign, CEO John Chambers realized that as the leader of the organization he had to play much more of an external role in promoting Cisco in the marketplace, even though his personality made him reluctant to take on this role:[10]

> Things have changed. And what has changed is the way that our company sold before was primarily a direct touch to large customers. And in that environment what you needed to do was make contact with the right decision makers in those customer environments and you had a direct operation that touched those customers. Now we're beginning to move more and more of our product through indirect channels and more and more of our product to medium and small accounts into the home, and so your importance of being visible as a company in the industry becomes very, very key to us. And unfortunately, the industry likes talking about the leader rather than the team that does it. And so therefore you see us become much more visible because while 80 or 90 percent of our products come out of large-enterprise customers today, that will probably be less than 50 percent within three years. ... And so the requirement for people asking for Cisco becomes very important. ... I'd rather spend time with customers or internally here than doing interviews or other things. However, having said that, that's now part of my job and responsibility, and it is an important part to our success. You can have the best products, the best service organization in the world, the best strategy, but if the products are being consumed indirectly and the people who are asking for the vendor selection don't know that, they aren't going to ask for Cisco. So it's something we're going to have to do more of that isn't particularly one of my top enjoyable things to do.

Internally, besides building systems to facilitate growth, the Accelerator has to ensure that growth isn't prematurely truncated by lack of managerial talent and depth in the organization. Rapid growth of the organization creates four major challenges in this area for the Accelerator. The first is growing the number of people as the organization grows while maintaining competence. The second is maintaining the ethic and culture of the organization, retaining the best of the entrepreneurial culture while adding people and structure. The third is in helping people who are in key positions to grow with the company and dealing with situations where these people are not able to grow their abilities at the speed the company is growing. Finally, the fourth major challenge is in retaining key people once the firm has climbed the growth path when these key people may be able to afford to retire because of their equity in the company, and when the company itself becomes a poaching ground for other growth companies.

The first major issue for many firms is in recruitment. For organizations that are growing at double-digit or even triple-digit rates, simply getting enough competent managers and employees through the door is a major concern. With such growth rates, it is impossible to promote solely from within, and so the organization is forced to look beyond its own boundaries for external talent. The question of where to look for these people and how to attract them in a small to medium-sized company is high on the priority list for many Accelerators. The CEO of a fast-growing distribution company faced this first challenge of growing the organization, providing a structure that allowed for continued growth and maintaining competence in key management:

> I'd say that right now, this is one of our major issues, you know, as to how can we grow a more professional managerial structure within the company. We've got some great people at the top, incredible work ethic, but you know, you're only going to get so far by your top two guys working until midnight every night. I mean, that's okay at a hundred million, maybe two hundred million in revenues. But this year our plan is for about three hundred million in revenue and the year after it'll probably be four hundred million and we're going to have to be doing things differently there to prosper, especially if we plan to expand into the rest of Europe and a second office in Paris serves a strategic role in that process.[11]

Maintaining the benefits of an entrepreneurial culture while trying to bring more structure to the organization is a very real challenge for Accelerators. There is a paradox of risk as the organization gets larger. On the one hand, when organization members take risks for the organization at the Creation stage, the risk can be great as bad decisions could potentially jeopardize the existence of the organization. However, such "bet the company" risks are often commonplace and necessary for survival at the early Growth phase. The paradox is that as the company gets larger, the same decisions less often jeopardize the company itself, but are often discouraged because of the growing feeling of having "something to lose" as the company gains in reputation and size. As a consequence, companies often devise rules and routines to minimize risk-taking and guide decision-making "by the book." While this may reduce errors and risks taken by the organization, it can also have a profound impact on the culture, beginning a process that may be seen by many in the organization as a descent into bureaucratization.

As the sports television network ESPN neared the end of its Growth phase, there was a noticeable shift in the culture from a risk-oriented, try anything value system to one where, as the network became the leader in sports broadcasting, the feeling developed that it had more to lose and so it became slightly more risk-averse. In the early days, during the Creation and early Growth phases, a new idea would be tried directly on air in prime-time, leading to potentially new innovations. For example, the concept of "cut-ins," where one sports game was interrupted by switching to another game during play, was developed during their coverage of the NCAA Basketball Tournament. ESPN faced tough decisions on which games were more important, and it decided to cut from one game to another, attempting to capture the great moments and more exciting games. The production staff were in a position where if this experiment didn't work, they just would not do it the next day. John Wildhack, a production executive at ESPN, told how the entrepreneurial spirit had softened at the production level since these earlier days:

> I think now, if we're going to try anything that's a little bit risky, we'll probably look at a certain time period, or a certain day, or a certain sport where we can maybe get away with it. If we want to test it on the air, in a sense, we'll pick our spots now and test it as opposed to just saying, "O.K. tomorrow we'll just do this." Now, the idea of young people being fearful of not doing the right thing for whatever reasons is difficult to avoid. Trying to reward risk-taking that is strategic and being cautious not to criticize when something does not succeed to the degree you thought it would. That's a real challenge of management.[12]

John Walsh, another ESPN executive, observed:

> I feel that we're at the point of the examination of style because the company is confronting the oxymoron in the workplace of the changing environment and the need for stabilization. The place has always been intimate; people have been dedicated to the work, often to the exclusion of things such as family and outside interests, but also to the exclusion of authority. One of management's challenges is to ask people to be aware of this shifting change at ESPN, because there has to be a higher value now on good judgment, on the respect for authority, the respect for each other, and the respect for one's time, without losing the positives of an entrepreneurial culture.[13]

One of the most difficult and painful tasks which the Accelerator has to deal with occurs when some of the key people who have helped to manage the organization as it has grown simply don't fit the new needs of the organization, or can't grow their managerial competence quickly enough to match the growth in the organization or the growth of their own responsibilities. Sometimes this can be remedied by training of one form or another, or in some cases, the person may be happy to return to a more technical job or manage a smaller part of the organization. However, frequently, none of these situations occurs and the Accelerator is left with the decision to remove responsibilities from a person who has been instrumental in helping the organization reach its current position, a loyal and a key member of the team, but currently out of his or her depth and holding the organization back. Jon Tompkins faced this situation more than once in his tenure as Accelerator CEO at semiconductor equipment supplier Tencor Instruments:

> All our key positions have really been filled when the company was $25 million to $50 million in size. So we've got people that we're asking to grow up very fast and manage $200 million operations when they were just a couple of years ago managing things one tenth of that size. How do you handle situations where the organization has grown so quickly that it's grown faster than very good, very competent people in certain roles? You come to a conclusion that you need somebody bigger, better, faster, or more experienced to be in that position for the company going forward but you really don't want to dump the person out on the street who has done this great job and worked as hard or as fast as he or she could and has.
>
> We have a good example in Korea. We went direct in Korea a year and a half ago. We thought at the time our business might someday be as large as $10 million, but we really had sort of a $5 million per year perspective. We hired a really good young sales manager. This guy is really good, but he's 10 years too young for the job of running a real company in Korea because he doesn't have the age stature that our customers expect. And the business exploded on us. We went from five people to more than twenty. We booked $38 million in Korea last year and will do the same this year. This guy has risen to the occasion in terms of booking the business, but he's just not old enough to get the relationships that we need to have now with Samsung, Hyundai and Gold Star. How do we get what we need without making this guy angry and driving him out of the company, which we absolutely don't want?[14]

Most fast-growth companies in the Growth phase will at some point face these development issues. Some companies approach the problem by adopting an up-or-out policy; people either grow and adapt as the company develops or they are dismissed. Other companies spend a lot of time, energy and money on working with and training their people so that most can grow with the company. Still others find a compromise approach, cross-training people and finding areas where they can still be valuable individual contributors while managing within their limitations. Two CEOs of high-tech companies have opposite approaches that they take with these development issues. The first company has a system of teams within the company that are responsible for individual projects. Each team is self-governing and has the responsibility for hiring and firing its own people, including recruiting new members from inside or outside the company. The CEO of that company uses an analogy to describe the de facto up-or-out policy of employment in the company:

> It's like you go down to the corner when you're trying to have a pick up game of basketball. You go down there every day, nobody picks you up, pretty soon you better go find something else – maybe go try baseball or something. Or go to a different league.[15]

However, the CEO of the second company takes the opposite approach, by making heavy investments in training and education for his team:

> If people don't know what they are doing, what good are they? And if you're not giving people an opportunity to grow and learn how to do the job better, what's the point? I am an educator. That's my deal. I've been doing it for a long, long time. I believe in it firmly. I think the success of our world depends upon education. People can only grow if they're educated.[16]

Companies in the Growth stage usually expend considerable energy and attention hiring people, with retention also a key issue, as companies do not wish to lose those people who have made a valuable contribution so far and already embody the culture of the organization, it being difficult enough to maintain a strong culture with a rapid influx of new people without losing those who already form the core of the culture. When a company is young and growing rapidly, yet still relatively small, it is able to poach people easily from larger companies with the lure of an exciting, challenging environment and the possible large payoff from the company going public in an IPO. However, when the company does go public, two factors could make retaining people more difficult: you have created paper millionaires who could quit and never work again; you emerge on the radar screen as a prime poaching ground for other companies, both large and small.

The millionaire issue, however, can be both a help as well as a hindrance. In one respect, there is the danger that people may leave and go off and do something else. John Tompkins, of Tencor Instruments, recognizes this possibility, citing the example of the former CEO of a company Tencor acquired:

> The wild card with Dave is that he made $12 million when we bought his company. It hasn't caused him to change his lifestyle yet, but someday he might wake up and say "Why am I doing this stuff?"[17]

The key to this issue, and the reason that not many companies suffer a mass exodus after an IPO, despite the obvious temptation of retiring and incentive mechanisms such as golden handcuffs imposed by the company, is that these type of people who are involved in growth companies prior to the IPO still believe in the vision of the company and are excited by the future – they don't see the IPO as marking the end of the journey towards the vision provided by the Creator, but merely a milestone marking progress towards that end. The CEO of a semiconductor manufacturer provided an example of how his company had managed to retain all its key people who profited out of its IPO:

> The first twenty-five people here – I'd say that not a single one of them doesn't have a net worth of less than $5 million at this point. The first twenty-five – not a single one of them has to work. They do it because they love it to death and because it's a great environment, they've got a lot of responsibility, a lot of authority, and in making the decisions, they call the shots.[18]

While there may be a temptation for some to leave on becoming IPO millionaires, Jon Tompkins of Tencor Instruments outlined the less obvious side of the paper millionaire coin; its secondary effect as an effective deterrent against a hostile takeover:

> Well, let's say we're talking about technology XYZ. If we don't have any of it and these five guys over here in this other company have it, we don't know these people. If you spend a bunch of money to buy it and they say "goodbye," and they're out the door, you are just left high and dry. If you're buying consumer products, clothing lines or whatever, you know, they are less individual sensitive kinds of businesses. It doesn't mean they are any easier. There are other things that drive success there. But high-tech companies have a high degree of people dependence.

But again, I think the real issue is that it's hard to do an unfriendly takeover of a real high-tech company because they're so people sensitive. In my case, if we were acquired in a hostile way, you know, you'd quickly think about do I want to be involved in that? I probably wouldn't.[19]

John Chambers, CEO of Cisco Systems, also pointed to a further benefit to the organization of financially independent paper millionaires:[20]

As people become financially independent, they actually are better leaders. They're more difficult to lead, but they will make the decisions for what they believe is right as opposed to because they've got to get this paycheck and they're going to keep their mouth shut even though they think there's a better way of doing it. So financial independence helps the company.

The key is how do you identify the next motivating point. How do you get your team to rally around changing the world, the way it works, lives, plays, and learns? How do you get your leaders rooted to their teams – because the number one reason a person leaves is, they see their leaders leave. One of the hardest things you do as a leader is to make changes in management; yet we all know that if you don't, you'll get your company into real serious trouble and your customers and your employees will suffer if you don't.

The issue of becoming a target of poaching by other firms seeking talent is often less one of money, and more one of challenge. The key people who are attracted to the young, exciting, high-growth companies in the Creation and Growth phases of the lifecycle, and those who the company does not want to lose, are the very people who are likely to be the first to leave for a new challenge if the environment in the company becomes a little stale, or even when the vision becomes a realizable accomplishment. Bill O'Mera of C-Cube Microsystems was resigned to this fact, but was using it as a stimulus or reminder that he needed to be constantly pushing the envelope:

Fact of life in Silicon Valley. It turns out that although money is important to all of us, it is almost always not the driving factor when people make job changes and why they go to company A versus company B. And so long as you are creating – we're providing the engineering talent in this company the opportunity to create something that doesn't exist. I mean, we're creating products that nobody else in the world has ever built before. We're not duplicating what somebody else has done. We're innovating. We're creating chips that nobody else has ever built, ever. And so it's a very challenging environment for the technical guys. And as long as we can keep them challenged, I think we'll be able to keep most of our good people. But we have lost people and we will continue to lose people to other start-ups.[21]

The success that a fast-growing company enjoys, particularly as the company grows in reputation and recognition in their peer community, while making the company a target for poaching talent, also has the effect of aiding retention through the intangible rewards people get from their association with the organization. The CEO of another semiconductor firm reinforced this point of challenge and success as being the key drivers in retaining top people:

> First you have to be a winner. Nobody's going to play on a losing team. And so far, we are winners. And it's painful sometimes, here working long hours, weekends, on projects trying to wrap them up, but at the end of the day, you know, their neighbors know who they are. They walk down the street and a lot of people know who they are, because they're associated with this company. They are designing semiconductors at this company. They are considered to be the best in the world. They are known and recognized. It feeds their ego.[22]

Finally, the Accelerator needs to continually monitor the mood of the organization and strike a balance between overconfidence and hubris creeping into the successful organization, and despair that can strike when momentum slows and seemingly insurmountable challenges occur that threaten the progress towards the realization of the organization's vision. John Chambers of Cisco Systems is constantly aware of this need to regulate the mood swings that can occur within the company:[23]

> There's always an intergalactical battle star about to destroy Cisco. And so, as unusual as this sounds, I actually jump back and forth from one side of the scale to the other. If our confidence starts to get a little too strong, I jump over to the paranoid side and say, here are all the things that can go wrong. If our confidence starts to shake a little, I jump over to the positive – here are all the things that can go right. I balance back and forth. And the time to change is when things are going well. So if you ever see us thinking we're invincible, that's the time to sell the stock, because we have lots of things that could trip us up and we know it. But it's that healthy paranoia and a willingness to address it that allows us to be successful.

The task of the Accelerator then is both an internal one as well as an external one. Externally, the constituents of the organization grow as the company grows and is successful in its marketplace, particularly if during the Growth phase the company takes the plunge of going public. Internally, there is not only the challenge of putting systems and routines in place to facilitate the growth of the organization, but the primary leadership role is one of managing the human resource challenges that come with growth, as the Accelerator struggles to maintain focus on the vision, develop the culture of the organization, and retain the excitement and enthusiasm of the entrepreneurial Creation phase.

The Accelerator's Leadership Style

Even within the Growth phase of the lifecycle, the probable leadership style of the Accelerator is apt to change. Just as the Creator tends to dominate the organization because of his or her embodiment of the vision for the organization, so in the early stages of the Growth phase, the Accelerator may also dominate because of his or her need to put in place a coherent system to deal with growth. Thus, in the early part of the Growth phase, we are likely to see an Accelerator who also takes most of the decisions and dominates the organization. However, as the Growth phase continues, and the role of the Accelerator becomes more external, and he or she becomes more of a face identified with the organization, on the inside he or she becomes less dominant and necessarily begins to decentralize decision-making in the organization.

In the *Fortune* magazine issue featuring the 100 fastest growing companies of 2000, the title of the article profiling Tom Siebel, CEO of Siebel Systems, was "Confessions of a Control Freak."[24] The article tells of how Tom Siebel has created a highly centralized company where "nothing is too insignificant to merit a rule." The detail orientation and degree of centralization and personal control by Siebel are reflected in the fact that until recently, even with sales approaching $1 billion annually, there were just four people who could authorize the hiring of staff and Siebel himself had to personally authorize any expenditure over $10,000. Siebel, first in the Creator and then in the Accelerator role, set out to build a highly professional, tightly run organization where, as *Fortune* described it, the modus operandi was "to create a company of lock-step uniformity where the rules matter more than who is in charge,"[25] where in every office around the world you would find the same color carpet, the same uniform gray desks, the same standard cubicles and offices. However, as Siebel Systems continued its rapid growth, Tom Siebel has shifted his style somewhat to loosen his direct grip on decision-making as he realized that continuing to micro-manage would restrict the organization's growth. He reflected: "I used to be the classic meddling entrepreneur who was convinced that I could do every job in the company better than everybody else, and I needed to demonstrate that."[26] Since then he has brought on a COO (chief operating officer) who has considerable authority and delegated more, without altering the company's fundamental culture and focus on his vision.

John Chambers is the third CEO at Cisco Systems, and the second to really take on the Accelerator role at the company. The company was founded by married co-Creators Leonard Bosack and Sandy Lerner, Stanford professors in computer science, and pioneers of Cisco's core product, the router. Their vision was for computers of all types to be connected to each other through a network and that Cisco would provide that network. As the company left the Creation phase and entered the Growth phase, John Morgridge took over as CEO of Cisco and became the first Accelerator, taking the company to a market capitalization of $9 billion before handing the reins over to John Chambers in 1995. John Chambers describes how the leadership style has changed and evolved through the Creation to early Growth to later Growth phases:[27]

> The second way I describe the culture is one that is going through multiple stages of leadership style. It was a typical founders' culture initially. Then we evolved out of the founders' crisis, and then had a new leadership group that focused on centralized management, where most of the decisions were made at the top, and organizations operated in funnels to the engineering group, the sales group, the service group. Now we're rapidly moving into decentralization and empowerment ... it's just the only way I know to grow the business at the pace we're going to grow. If all the decisions have to come to the top to get made, you slow it down too much.

These two examples demonstrate the range of styles that an Accelerator may take, but also show the overall trend that as the company accelerates through the Growth phase, the appropriate style tends to move from a more centralized to a less centralized approach.

Transition from Growth to Maturity Phase

As the organization reaches the end of the Growth phase of the lifecycle, the high rates of growth experienced by the organization begin to taper off as market saturation is approached. It becomes harder and harder, and requires more and more resources, to gain each point of market share. Competition becomes more fierce, and the focus switches from an internal one of installing systems and processes to cope with growth, to an external one focused on the competition. The growth phase is an exciting one for the organization, often characterized by rapid promotions and increasing responsibilities for organization members, and the constant addition of new staff. If the company goes public during this phase, excitement is generated by the progress of the company's stock, and eyes can become glued to the ticker symbol. As the growth tapers off and the company enters the Maturity phase of the lifecycle, the leadership role transitions from one of containing excitement to maintaining excitement as the natural slowdown in growth means slower promotions, less rapid change, a greater focus on evolutionary rather than revolutionary improvements in processes, and a change in orientation of the firm from one engaged in a sprint to the slower pace of the unending marathon.

Notes

1. Why John Chambers is the CEO of the future. *Chief Executive*, July 2000. pp. 27–36, p. 29.
2. Cisco CEO opens up on challengers. *Network World*, October 6, 1997, pp. 12, 134, p. 134.
3. Nee, Eric. 1996. An interview with John Chambers. *Upside*, July pp. 54–69, pp. 60–1.
4. LaPlante, Alice, 1997. The man behind Cisco. *Electronic Business*, December 1997, pp. 48–53, p. 50.
5. Ibid. pp. 50–51.
6. Interview with author.
7. Interview with author.
8. Interview with author.
9. Interview with author.
10. See note 3, pp. 66–7.
11. Interview with author.
12. Interview with author.
13. Interview with author.
14. Interview with author.
15. Interview with author.
16. Interview with author.
17. Interview with author.
18. Interview with author.
19. Interview with author.
20. See note 1, pp. 27–36, p. 36.
21. Interview with author.
22. Interview with author.
23. See note 1, pp. 27–36, p. 36.
24. Warner, Melanie. 2000. Confessions of a control freak. *Fortune*, September 4, pp. 130–40.
25. Ibid, p. 132.
26. Ibid, p. 138.
27. See note 3, p. 64.

CHAPTER 4

The Sustainer

Sustainers maintain the forward momentum of the organization, but position the organization for the long haul. As the organization goes through the Maturity phase of the lifecycle, the strategic focus shifts to one of market dominance, fighting to increase the organization's share of the market. Inevitably, as the organization succeeds in growing its market share, the increments by which it does so decrease, and each market share point becomes harder and harder to acquire. As the organization begins to struggle over tenths of a point of market share, the Sustainer's primary challenge becomes one of keeping excitement and motivation in the organization. No longer is the organization in a sprint as it was in the Growth phase, it has now settled into the grind of a never-ending marathon, and maintaining the organization's energy and vitality is an increasingly difficult task. With its worldwide reach and over a century of history behind it, The Coca-Cola Company epitomizes an organization that has been able to sustain itself from generation to generation in an extended Maturity phase, yet is able to keep excited about its future prospects for growth and an awareness of the dangers of complacency brought on by success. Douglas Daft, Chairman and CEO of The Coca-Cola Company, captures the essence of the Sustainer role:

> To be excited about the future, we simply have to look at the vast opportunity before us throughout the world. Every day, there are people who are only now enjoying their first Coke. For millions of other consumers, we are providing them Coca-Cola or other beverages they desire.
>
> We simply cannot fall into the traps of complacency and hubris. And we know it! We must appreciate the hard work and brilliance of generation after generation of men and women whose vision and successful execution built the busi-

ness from which we all today benefit. Optimizing the existing strengths of our company – and securing those strengths for future generations – is the road to our continued success. We know the road is tougher today than ever before. Competition is more intense, markets are more complex, consumers more demanding. As a result, complacency or hubris has no place in our company. Simply stated, we are never satisfied, we cannot rest![1]

To achieve this, the Sustainer must keep the organization focused on the vision of the company and continually keep the vision both consistent and fresh as the organization changes over time. The immediate danger is that in order to keep the organization constantly on its toes, the Sustainer may be tempted to generate false crises within the organization, trying to make it respond to danger that is not really an imminent threat. In doing so, the Sustainer can succumb to the fate of the legendary "boy who cried wolf." Companies in the Maturity phase of the lifecycle are not undergoing revolutionary change, but those that sustain success are constantly seeking evolutionary changes needed to improve efficiency and adjust to prevailing conditions. Peter Brabeck, CEO of Swiss food giant Nestlé, underlines this fundamental truth and tells how Nestlé avoids crying wolf:

> Big, dramatic change is fine for a crisis. If you come in as CEO and a turn-around is necessary, then fine, have a revolution. In that situation, change is relatively easy because the whole organization understands that, just to survive, you need to do things differently. They are prepared for change. They understand when you say, "The cancer is here, where do I cut?"

> But not every company in the world is in crisis all the time. Many companies are like us – not as big, of course – but they are performing well. Growing, innovating, and so forth – good and fit. Why should we manufacture dramatic change? Just for change's sake? To follow some sort of fad without logical thinking behind it? We are very skeptical of any kind of fad and of the self-appointed gurus you hear from all the time, making pronouncements. It's easy to be dogmatic when you don't actually have to run a business. When you run a business, you must be pragmatic. Big, disruptive change programs are anything but that. You cannot underestimate the traumatic impact of abrupt change, the distraction it causes in running the business, the fear it provokes in people, the demands it makes on management's time.

> And frankly, you could make the case that any kind of one-time change program is actually a very worrisome warning – it's a bad sign that a company's leaders have had to make such an intervention. Think of medicine again. If you take preventative care of your health, and you've taken the time

for check-ups, you won't wake up one day to find you have to cut off your leg. That is why we see adapting, improving, and restructuring as a continuous process. ... Evolution can happen if you believe in it. You can have slow and steady change, and that is nothing to be ashamed of. Our market capitalization in 1997 was CHF 55 billion [Swiss Francs], and today it is around CHF 150 billion. It happened without frenzy, without bloodshed. Just constantly challenging people to be better, day by day, bit by bit.

(Reprinted by permission of *Harvard Business Review*. Excerpt from "The Business Case Against Revolution: An Interview with Nestlé's Peter Brabeck" by Wetlaufer, Suzy, February 2001. Copyright © 2001 by the Harvard Business School Publishing Corporation; all rights reserved.)

Another reason that large organizations in the Maturity phase of the lifecycle focus on evolutionary change rather than disruptive revolutions is that the key to incrementally building market share is gaining the trust of their market, such that consumers can rely on the organization and its products. This level of trust is particularly paramount where breaking that trust can cause actual harm to consumers, such as drug companies, or those in the food and beverage industries. It is why maintaining and rebuilding that trust becomes the number one priority if something goes wrong. While companies are susceptible to external terrorism which can precipitate a crisis and damage trust, despite any preventive measures they may take, such as Johnson & Johnson suffered in 1982 and 1986 with tampering of Tylenol, there is only so much a company can do to anticipate such a crisis, and if the company responds responsibly, trust can be restored when consumers realize that the incident was externally caused. However, consumers' trust can also be damaged by changes made by the company, as The Coca-Cola Company discovered when they reformulated Coca-Cola in 1985, replacing it with New Coke. Despite taste tests showing that the taste of New Coke was preferred over both Coca-Cola and Pepsi, the company had overlooked the strong consumer attachment to the original formula, which was held by many to be beyond just a softdrink and part of the fabric of America. Protests and outcries ensued, with more than 1,000 protesters' phone calls a day pouring into Coca-Cola's hotline, together with bagfuls of mail with comments such as "I don't think I would be more upset if you were to burn the flag in our front yard,"[2] and one addressed to Chairman and CEO Roberto Goizueta as "Dear Chairman Dodo."[3] Less than three months after replacing Coca-Cola with New Coke, the company capitulated and reintroduced the original formula as Coca-Cola Classic. In the commercial that told the world of Coca-Cola's return, Don Keough, Coca-Cola's President, explained that the company's strategy was being changed in response to the consumer:

I'm Don Keough, President of The Coca-Cola Company. When we brought you the new taste of Coke, we knew that millions would prefer it. And millions do. And we knew that it would beat the taste of our major competitor. And it does. What we didn't know was how many thousands of you would phone and write asking us to bring back the classic taste of original Coca-Cola. Well, we read, and we listened. And you know the rest. They're both yours – the new taste of Coke and Coca-Cola Classic. Your right of choice is back.

By listening and responding to consumer demands in this way, Coca-Cola was not only able to recapture consumer trust, but it ended up as a positive event for the company by making people realize their identity with the brand and the drink, revitalizing Coca-Cola Classic's sales. When you have an established organization and brand, and in Coca-Cola's case, the most valuable brand in the world[4] and one that has endured for over a century, the Sustainer's primary responsibility is essentially being entrusted with maintaining and carrying forward that legacy for the next generation. Douglas Daft, current Chairman and CEO of The Coca-Cola Company, articulates this challenge:

> We have inherited the responsibility for a great company and must leave it to those who follow with all the vibrancy, energy and creativity it has exhibited throughout its history. We have to stay true to those values that have made The Coca-Cola Company what it is today: the commitment is always to listen to our consumers, and the discipline never to rest on our laurels.[5]

Peter Brabeck of Nestlé echoes the importance of this trust relationship and how radical change within the organization can destroy it:

> Nestlé caters to billions of consumers around the world. In our business – food and drink – more perhaps than in others, we need a relationship of trust to be successful. Can anyone trust a company that reinvents itself every few years? Sure, we will act swiftly to change our products and our business methods if need be, and we do our best to improve all aspects of the company each day. But we will never allow our value system, or our focus on quality and safety, to deteriorate. Trust is our most important asset. We must always defend it.

> That's why I think one of the main jobs of the leader is to determine what aspects of the company you want to keep. You have to be clear about why the company has been successful in the past, and how you're going to keep those fundamentals from breaking down or disappearing.

Inevitably, as the organization grows to a state of maturity, and that period is sustained for a considerable length of time, the environment in which the company operates changes. As these changes occur, particularly if the company endures over decades, the challenge for the Sustainer is to keep the vision of the organization relevant. Because of the success of the organization, its vision has been kept clearly in focus, and so the Sustainer is not there to throw out the vision and bring in an entirely new vision. However, the Sustainer needs to be aware of how the environment has changed and be able to update the vision while maintaining the spirit of the organization's original mission. Sustainers, then, focus on constantly refining the organization through evolutionary change, which sometimes includes adjusting the overall mission to fit the changing environment but without straying from the organization's core vision. As Don Keough, former President of The Coca-Cola Company, told students at Duke University, there is a constant need for vigilance and readjusting the mission as befits the situation:

> In 1981 one of the first things Roberto Goizueta and I did as the newly elected Chairman and President of The Coca-Cola Company was to assemble the Company's worldwide top management team for a strategy session. At that meeting we developed a global mission statement for the 1980's which set forth our agreed upon goals and objectives and the strategies for achieving our mission.

> In the mid-80's we revised our mission statement and strategies. Out of those sessions came statements which were communicated to every employee at every level in the worldwide Coca-Cola system.

> In the decade of the 80's and early 90's we managed The Coca-Cola Company according to the plan we had developed – according to the mission. But we were not rigid and unchanging. We recognized the need to constantly re-evaluate and change our strategy to meet the fast changing business climate.

> That is why it is so important for a leader to constantly reconceptualize the activities and events of an organization – in effect, the mission – cut through the clutter of a complex situation and simplify it so that everyone understands where we are going. Bureaucracies, by their nature, tend to complicate things. A leader needs to simplify things. And that is not easy.[6]

The companies that achieve enduring success and are able to maintain a dominance in their maturity phase for decades and over successive generations of Sustainer leadership demonstrate a great consistency in being able to take the legacy of the original vision and constantly focus on applying it to the changing business climate. Some two decades after

Don Keough assumed the Presidency of The Coca-Cola Company, a new generation of leaders at the company, led by Douglas Daft still maintains this unwavering focus:

> To know where one is going, one needs to know where one has been. Remembering and honoring our past is more than a nostalgic exercise, it is also a guide to the future. Great companies don't chase after the latest fad or change their strategic direction on a whim. They are not easily distracted. They understand the promise of market position and market opportunity, remaining single-mindedly concentrated on what they do best – and on doing it better each day.

> At the same time, great companies continually foster inventiveness. So yes, great organizations must and do change, just as the world around them changes. Great companies see the value of advanced technology and employ it creatively to increase efficiency, speed, and cost-effectiveness. They look for innovative and new ways to serve their customers and consumers, some of which extend beyond traditional boundaries and business models. At the heart of inventiveness is a willingness to question whether what worked phenomenally well yesterday is still the right approach for tomorrow. That's why at The Coca-Cola Company, we believe we are just half way through a 200-year business plan.[7]

Another example of an organization that has managed to maintain its dominance over many decades and generations of Sustainers is provided by United Parcel Service (UPS). It was founded by Jim Casey in 1907 as the American Messenger Company, delivering notes, hand-baggage, and packages by foot, streetcar, or bicycle. Despite these humble beginnings, the core values of the company in terms of how it operated and the service and value it provided, summarized by Casey's slogan, "Best Service and Lowest Rates," were maintained throughout the decades that followed. Always a humble organization, reflecting its founder's values, it was some eight decades later that UPS finally aired its first advertisements on television. The first ad captured the essence of what UPS was about and how the core values of UPS remained the same even through the many changes the organization had gone through in the meantime. The commercial began by showing old black and white photographs of early UPS trucks and bicycles, and spoke of the founding of the company by Jim Casey back in 1907, which then transitioned into film of UPS's modern aircraft fleet and information technology transporting packages and next-day air letters, as an old recording of founder Jim Casey spoke in the background. "We'll provide the best service for the lowest rates, because we'll hustle where others dawdle. We'll keep our bicycles well oiled. We'll have no fat in our system and none in our prices." A new voice then explained that "Jim Casey proved that when you run at peak efficiency you not only perform a better service, but you have the luxury of charging less for it. And that's why today, UPS can deliver next-day air letters usually for half what less efficient companies charge." The commercial concluded with the slogan, "UPS. We run the tightest ship in the shipping business."

In one 30-second sound bite, UPS had demonstrated how they have translated their founding vision to keep it relevant and how it still served as the heart of the company. The bicycles may have changed to aircraft, but the underlying concept of keeping them running as a well-oiled machine still resonates within the company today as much as it did in 1907.

The Sustainer's Organization

During the Growth phase of the lifecycle, the challenge for the Accelerator is putting systems in place to allow the organization to grow. As the organization reaches the Maturity phase of the lifecycle, the systems and routines the organization needs to be successful are in place, and the focus is on constantly refining those systems to maximize efficiency as the organization pursues scale and market share. Like many companies in the Maturity phase of the lifecycle, UPS's traditional emphasis has been on replicating what has been successful and eliminating errors from the systems, constantly refining their processes down to the smallest detail. For example, its "340 methods" for drivers spells out exactly how they are to go about their routine, down to details such as how they are to carry the truck keys to avoid fumbling and unnecessary movement.

However, as a company sustains its success over a prolonged period, and systems are refined to generate maximum efficiency, the tendency is for the organization to become obsessive about efficiency and begin instituting rules and procedures for every detail. While the goal of increasing efficiency is a noble one and not in itself detrimental for an organization, it has two related dangers that the Sustainer needs to guard against. The first is that the routines and procedures promote a tendency towards the status quo. While, in some regard, this is what the organization is after in instituting these practices which are designed to enable it to replicate past success, it often comes at the cost of stifling innovation. Indeed, the mindset of efficiency and the status quo can begin to creep into the reward system of the organization, beginning to reward people for upholding the way things are and maintaining a steady state and discouraging people from sticking their necks out for creative solutions to problems. The related danger is that while the pursuit of perfect efficiency is fine in a stable environment, the ingrained, rigid rules and procedures can reduce the organization's ability to adapt to a changing environment. Thus the Sustainer's challenge is to balance the need for efficiency which promotes competitiveness in the current environment, while maintaining the organization's ability to rewrite its rules and procedures in order to retain its competitiveness when conditions change. This is the quintessential dilemma for large, mature organizations, which, like large ships, are by their very nature more efficient but more difficult to maneuver than smaller vessels.

The Sustainer's Task

Given this dilemma for organizations in the Maturity phase of the life-cycle, which can last many decades and generations of leaders, the Sustainer's task is to maintain this balance between efficiency and nimbleness, and adapt the vision of the organization as the needs of the environment change, while maintaining the essence of the organization's original vision.

In maintaining the balance between the efficiency which comes from well-defined rules and procedures and the nimbleness which comes from the ability to make decisions and implement them quickly, the Sustainer of a mature company usually has to work harder at promoting the latter while harnessing the former in order to maintain the balance. The way in which the Sustainer can achieve this balance is by nurturing a culture or mindset that embraces change, which is very difficult to do in any organization, let alone one that is naturally prone to maintaining the status quo as it seeks to replicate its past success. One of the ways that the Sustainer can build and nurture a culture that embraces change is to look to the history of the organization itself and use symbols, images, stories and legends of behavior which encapsulate how the organization has embraced change in the past. Shortly after Carly Fiorina took over as CEO of Hewlett-Packard in 1999, she introduced a $200 million advertising campaign which was aimed as much internally to the organization as it was externally to customers. The focus of the campaign was on the original "one-car garage in need of paint"[8] where Bill Hewlett and Dave Packard had founded the company 60 years earlier. The image was meant to convey, as Fiorina put it, that Hewlett-Packard is "a company founded by inventors, fuelled by invention and adept at reinventing ourselves to track new market opportunities."[9] In launching this campaign, Fiorina was trying to both refocus the company on its heritage, getting it back to the original vision of the organization, and exemplify how the founders were adept at change and that the politics and stifling bureaucracy which had engulfed Hewlett-Packard had no place in a garage-like entrepreneurial environment that she hoped to bring back to the company.

In a similar way, Jim Kelly used his chairman's letter to shareholders in UPS's first annual report as a public company, having gone public in November 1999, to convey that, although going public was one of many profound changes occurring at the company, change was nothing new to UPS:

> I should also point out that today's changing environment is nothing new to UPS. Transformation and reinvention are a way of life for us. Since our humble beginnings in a small basement office in Seattle, UPS has refined the art of changing to keep ahead of new market realities, new competitors, new technologies, and new models for conducting business and enabling commerce.
>
> There are certain timeless values and philosophies that define our culture at UPS. Indeed, I believe the extraordinary dedication of our people, and the strong commitments we make to our customers, shareowners, and communities are the primary reasons we have been able to grow our business for nearly a century.
>
> Our people and our values are also why we are now poised to enable our customers' move into a new frontier of commerce as we begin the next century.

Two years later, Kelly expanded on this notion and particularly how the culture had been remolded to allow the company to recognize that change is a part of who they are and so allow them to embark on a course of future change:

> The truth, really, is that we've reinvented ourselves many times. But that wasn't a fact that our people reflected on. It's something we've only recently started thinking about. As we have wrestled with uncertainty in many areas of our business – technology investments, global competitors' moves, and so on – it has been helpful to remind ourselves that uncertainty has existed in our history many, many, many times. I mentioned, for example, that we found success as a delivery consolidator for retail stores in the 1930s. Well, that business completely dried up with the advent of shopping malls after World War II,

and we were compelled to create a new business. So we reinvented ourselves as a common-carrier wholesale business, competing with the postal service – something that had never been done before. We subsequently created an airline to provide next-day service, and we moved from serving three countries to serving 200 – within a year, and by ourselves.

My point is that, in the last three to five years, we've begun talking about our history in this way to give ourselves a sense of "Yeah, it's new and it's different, and it's tough and it's a change – but that's okay. We've done that successfully for many years." The new UPS charter I mentioned was unveiled in 1998, and the value of innovation is prominent in it. We've built the same message into our external and internal communications. And, as a result, we've given ourselves a little more confidence that we're able to do what we have to do.

Part of the challenge of adjusting the vision to adapt to changing times while keeping the essence of the vision the same is in balancing how far from the core business the company should wander in order to enable growth without diminishing the central focus of the organization. While UPS had begun in its early days as the American Messenger Company, delivering messages as well as packages and even food from restaurants, the core business had developed over the decades as primarily a package delivery company. However, as the company matured and grew over the decades, and reached the point of a global package delivery service, other areas were needed in order to continue to grow. Jim Kelly described this process of diversifying but maintaining the core vision:

We know we need to reach far beyond our core business, but in ways that respect and complement it. A few years ago, we undertook an effort to rethink our mission and charter. Instead of seeing ourselves as just a package delivery business, we defined our purpose more broadly as enabling global commerce. It's certainly true: We serve 8 million shippers and receivers a day and move about 6% of the U.S. G.D.P. But global commerce involves a lot more than moving goods; it's just as much about moving information and money. So now we think in terms of all three of those flows as we create broader offerings for our customers and push deeper and deeper into their supply chains. The fastest growing part of UPS today is our logistics business, which involves our taking over logistics management activities from shippers. We also offer global financing services to new and expanding businesses through our UPS Capital business.

Revamping our mission clarified how our new undertakings fit with what we have done well in the past. Take consolidation, for example. One of the things Jim

Casey, our founder, did in the early days of UPS was to convince retailers, all of whom had their own delivery trucks, to let us perform that function for them. This was a huge step at the time – the idea that your merchandise would be placed on a truck alongside your competitors'. Today, one of the elements in our logistics group is Service Parts Logistics; we keep a spare parts inventory and make deliveries of critical parts as well as perform warranty repair services for companies like Lexmark and Dell. Because we can offer this service in an end-of-runway facility, with technicians working overnight, our clients can provide much faster service to their own customers. But again, it's a question of convincing technology companies to place their inventories in the same facilities – staffed by the same people, using the same technology – as their competitors'. We face the same challenge Jim Casey did: to convince customers that a particular function is not central to their competitive advantage and can be better performed by us.

While UPS managed to grow through broadening its focus in its offerings without straying from the core mission of the organization, the Girl Scouts addressed the issue of lack of growth by broadening its reach through redefining what was meant by the original mission of the organization. The Girl Scouts had been founded by Juliette Gordon Low on March 12, 1912 in Savannah, Georgia, where she dreamed of giving the United States "something for all the girls,"[10] bringing them out of their home environments to serve their communities and experience the open air. Since that time it has grown into an organization of 233,000 troops and groups in the United States and in 81 countries through Girl Scouts Overseas, with 2.8 million girl members in the U.S. aged between 5 and 17. Marsha Johnson Evans, a retired rear admiral in the U.S. Navy, took over the leadership of the Girl Scouts in 1998 and saw that while the organization had been highly successful, becoming what she termed an "iconic organization" with enormous respect throughout the country, it was largely comfortable as an organization and missing the opportunity to serve girls in many different groups:

When I came into the organization, it was a sound organization from the point of view of the financial statements. A good endowment, a revenue stream that was very predictable – a significant portion of revenue coming from membership dues and from the proceeds from sales of uniforms, badges, handbooks and all of the other girl scout paraphernalia. And then interest on the fund. Indeed there had been a pattern of budgetary surpluses each year for a number of years when I arrived. And 11% of all the girls in the United States were Girl

Scouts. So when I arrived there was a sense that things were going well, that the organization was quite on track. But there were clues for me – in the search process I asked about my role in fund raising and was told that there was no need to raise money because the finances were really on track from those revenue streams.

So I came into the organization and immediately was struck by the fact – and the membership hadn't been growing over the years – so I was struck by the fact that when you asked the second question on the membership data, you know, what percentage of different population groups, whether you cut the data by rural/urban/suburban, or you cut it by racial/ethnic or however you chose to analyze the data, there were huge disparities in serving girls in different categories of the population. And quite frankly, there wasn't a lot of concern about that. There wasn't an imperative that this issue had to be addressed, even though at the time the stated corporate goal included three words: leadership, values and diversity. Diversity was in the picture of corporate goals, but not really on the radar horizon. Diversity was really more on the composition of the staff, and we have an exceptionally diverse staff. So I found it very interesting, and concluded very early on that something would have to happen to take the organization out of its comfort zone and to create an imperative to address the disparity in how we serve girls.

One of the things I learned over time was what an opportunity there was to anchor that reorientation in the original vision statement of the founder, at that point about 85 years before. She said, "I have something for all the girls." I still say in my speeches, "She didn't say 'All the girls that could conveniently get to meetings,' she didn't say 'All the girls whose parents are convinced it's a really good idea,' she didn't say, 'All the girls that have the resources to pay the membership dues, buy the handbook and buy the uniform.' She meant all the girls, and she said that."[11]

So Evans used the initial vision of the founder as an organization for "all the girls" to refocus the organization on expanding its reach to the underserved demographic groups where Girl Scouts had historically not had a large following and had not focused their efforts. This refocusing of the vision of the organization necessitated both an internal and an external change; to change the perceptions of those inside the organization as to who their constituencies were, and the perceptions of girls and parents of underserved demographic groups who hadn't previously considered the Girl Scouts as an option. However, before the external change in perception could be attempted, the internal change had to be made. Evans commented:

It's a huge internal change, and that became very apparent right away, because I don't think people appreciated the fact that the first change had to come from how we see ourselves. Only then could we extend that vision outward. So we worked very hard on the internal point of view first.[12]

Making the internal changes, however, was not as simple as just restating and communicating a new vision, but required a substantial change in both processes and orientation. While most people accepted the new vision and how it could revitalize the organization, the challenge lay in the implementation. With that implementation came a substantial change in the staffing of the organization as different skills were required to put the vision into action. As Evans described it:

Once we began articulating the fact that we'd got to do better, there were people who got it right away. Now, what also becomes difficult is you may get it in your heart, but then when you try to do it, it's really hard, because it requires more resources. So associated with the change in language about how well we're doing and what work there is to be done also came a commitment from the national administration, from myself, that we would also step up what is now a pretty robust fundraising effort, and that one of the things we had to do was to take on that issue of finding the resources. That was frankly pretty gut-wrenching because what it meant was that I had to change the staff functions, I had to stop doing some things that we were doing and reorient and redirect those resources.[13]

Thus, even though the organization was in the maturity stage and functioning well by their own yardsticks, there was still a need to adapt the vision to a changing environment, in this case a changing demographic shift in their potential audience. Making such a shift, even when it is seemingly a very minor change in interpreting the vision of the organization, can be difficult to implement in a mature organization. However, to maintain growth and the relevance of the organization, periodic shifts are necessary. Indeed, within two years of the internal initiative to broaden the focus of the Girl Scouts, membership in targeted demographic groups was growing significantly as the organization was able to shift to changing the external perception of the Girl Scouts.

The two tasks of the Sustainer to maintain the balance between efficiency and nimbleness and to adjust the vision to the changing context are not entirely separate activities, but in fact are fundamentally linked. An organization cannot adapt its vision appropriately to changing times, keeping the core of the vision intact, without balancing the benefits of the core systems already in place with the changes needed as market demands shift. On the other side of the coin, a relentless focus on the central mission of the organization facilitates appropriate change when it needs to shift its processes in order to accomplish its vision in a new environment. John Sawhill, CEO of the Nature Conservancy until his death in May 2000, explained how this interlinking facilitated change in the context of his organization, explaining first the vision of the Nature Conservancy, how it discovered that the way it was being implemented was failing and how the organization could adjust to a new strategy for implementing the same core vision:

> The Conservancy has always had a very clear mission: to preserve plants and animals and special habitats that represent the diversity of life. We are completely focused on that mission; it drives everything we do. We had to change though, because while we were doing a lot of good conservation work, there were more and more signs that we were not making significant progress towards accomplishing our mission.

> Our mission hasn't changed. Our approach has. You might call our original approach a Noah's Ark strategy. For four decades, the Conservancy focused almost exclusively on setting aside critical habitats for endangered species. In practice, that meant buying the specific piece of wetlands, forest, or prairie that supported a particular species or natural community. Like Noah, the Conservancy was intent on building an ark – or, more accurately, building a lot of little arks. ... We thought we could buy a piece of land, fence it off, and thereby protect whatever was in that preserve. But that thinking proved mistaken, which meant that our old performance measures – such as how much land we had acquired for conservation – weren't valid indicators of institutional progress.

> We simply couldn't go on with business-as-usual. For-profit companies can look at their financial statements every day to see how they're doing: They're either making money or not. Without the discipline of the bottom line, it's easier for nonprofit organizations to get off track. For the Conservancy, science is really our bottom line.

> And science led us to our new strategy. It became clear that we needed to influence land use in larger areas surrounding the kinds of core preserves that we had traditionally acquired. Now we focus on much larger landscapes, areas we call Last Great Places. That way we can work to ensure that the economic and recreational activities going on outside the preserves don't undermine the balance of life inside them. ...

People in this organization are deeply committed to its mission. They care about it; they think about it all the time. Fundamentally, it's what drives them. There is something about a nonprofit's mission that motivates people by closely aligning personal values with professional values. Maybe there's a lesson here for corporations. When mission comes first, people are more open to change: They accept changes that would probably cause a lot of anxiety if they weren't committed to the larger purpose. We invested an enormous amount of time and energy in the strategy process, and once we got it done, our people generally accepted the changes. They were convinced that the new strategy was the right way to achieve our mission.

(Reprinted by permission of *Harvard Business Review*. Excerpt from "Surviving Success: An Interview with The Nature Conservancy's John Sawhill" by Howard, Alice and Magretta, Joan, Sep–Oct 1995. Copyright © 1995 by the Harvard Business School Publishing Corporation; all rights reserved.)

The Sustainer's Leadership Style

In managing a mature organization, particularly a large one, the Sustainer's style needs to be participative, coupled with the ability to decentralize and delegate decision-making. The systems for operating the company are largely in place, and the scale of the organization means that centralizing decision-making could easily end up paralyzing the organization and would not allow the Sustainer to maintain the balance between efficiency and nimbleness. Indeed, both would suffer. Instead of focusing on making detailed decisions, the Sustainer needs to focus on the larger picture, ensuring that the vision and strategy for the organization remain consistent with the competitive dynamic of the company's markets and ensuring that the organization is constantly aligned with this mission. As Robert Haas, Chairman of jeans giant Levi Strauss & Co., puts it:

> If companies are going to react quickly to changes in the marketplace, they have to put more and more accountability, authority, and information into the hands of the people who are closest to the products and the customers. That requires new business strategies and different organizational structures. But structure and strategy aren't enough.

> This is where values come in. In a more volatile and dynamic business environment, the controls have to be conceptual. They can't be human anymore: Bob Haas telling people what to do. It's the ideas of a business that are controlling, not some manager with authority. Values provide a common language for aligning a company's leadership and its people.[14]

Ensuring that the values are consistent across the organization requires the Sustainer to spend a lot of time communicating the vision to the organization and explaining the strategy so that everyone is moving in the same direction. Jim Kelly of UPS explained this need and the challenge of doing this in a large organization:

> We have over 360,000 people operating in 200 countries and territories, and one of our biggest challenges is simply getting them to understand our strategy. We have plenty of communications processes and an organization that is generally willing to respond, but there's no getting around the fact that it takes time. People need a pretty good understanding of the company's strategy, not just some superficial phrases, if they're going to move together in the right direction.
>
> (Reprinted by permission of *Harvard Business Review*. Excerpt from "Reinvention with Respect. An Interview with Jim Kelly of UPS" by Kirby, Julia, November 2001. Copyright © 2001 by the Harvard Business School Publishing Corporation; all rights reserved.)

Transition from Maturity to Decline Phase

When an organization has been in the maturity phase for a long time and enjoyed sustained success, particularly if it has achieved a dominant position within its market, it is difficult constantly to keep the balance between striving for efficiency in a steady state and retaining nimbleness to adapt to change. Generally, sustained success tilts the balance towards maintaining the company's current processes in order to replicate success. However, in going down this road, the tendency is for bureaucracy creep to occur as rules and procedures become fossilized and essentially written in stone so that the rule itself becomes more important than what the rule was intended to produce. In concert with this bureaucracy creep, a heroic self-concept grows within the organization that prevents it from questioning the rigid imposition of rules. This heroic self-concept is a hubris that develops in the organization due to its success in the past which builds the notion of infallibility into the organization and a belief in the processes of the organization, such that no alternative processes or solutions, particularly those developed outside the organization, can be viable and must, almost by definition, be inferior to those that the organization currently uses. This heroic self-concept promotes bureaucracy creep and a rigidity in the processes of the organization so that it loses its ability to adapt and respond to changing conditions and any nimbleness that the organization had is lost. Consequently, as the environmental conditions which the organization faces begin to change, particularly if the shift is not radical but incremental, such that decline occurs slowly, the organization slips into the Decline phase of the lifecycle.

Whereas slipping into a state of declining performance can prove almost instantly fatal to smaller organizations, larger, more established organizations can often "rest on their laurels," or drift into a state of hubris and subsequent declining performance for quite some time. Indeed, Marshall Meyer and Lynne Zucker have identified what they describe as a phenomena of "permanently failing organizations," which are those normally large and at one time successful organizations, "whose performance, by any standard, falls short of the expectations of owners, members, and clients, yet whose existence continues, sometimes indefinitely."[15] These organizations are cushioned for a long time by the capital built up in periods of sustained success in the Maturity phase, and thus can survive seemingly permanently despite lagging performance.

When companies begin to perform poorly, an interesting dynamic occurs which can serve to further fossilize the processes of the organization. Meyer and Zucker contend that as organizational performance declines, the divergent interests of owners, managers, employees, and other organizational dependents, such as suppliers, can cause the sustenance of poor performance while sustaining the organization itself. As performance declines and the residual interest of owners also declines, their propensity for risk increases as they have little left to lose, and much to gain. However, for those who are more dependent on the organization's existence for their livelihood, particularly employees, and also suppliers and other dependents, the increased risk of failure of the organization from declining performance decreases their propensity for risk. Thus they are less willing to take risks to turn performance around since outright failure is more costly to them than the benefits derived from increasing performance beyond a level that sustains the organization and their livelihood. Indeed, some contributors to poor organizational performance, such as excess wages or perks, or failure to keep up with the latest techniques and knowledge in the industry, further reduce the ability or incentive for employees to switch organizations and this increases their risk aversion still further, but strengthens their motivation to keep the organization alive. With a high level of risk aversion, organizations become unwilling to adapt new technologies and routines and drop into a vicious circle of declining performance.

In some theoretical senses, in particular those from an ecological perspective, this is very inefficient in economic terms, as in a theoretically perfect marketplace, dysfunctionally performing firms should be instantly replaced by more efficient and competitive organizations. However, the fact that past success has allowed the build-up of sufficient capital to avoid financial disaster for a considerable period provides them with a window of opportunity for transformation between the onset of declining performance and the ending of the organization. This window provides the opportunity for a Transformer to reverse the vicious circle and revive the fortunes of the organization.

Notes

1. Interview with author.
2. Greising, David. 1998. *I'd Like the World to Buy a Coke: The Life and Leadership of Roberto Goizueta*. New York: John Wiley & Sons, p. 132.
3. Ibid.
4. The world's 10 most valuable brands. Business Week/Interbrand Ranking. *Business Week*, August 6, 2001.
5. Interview with author.
6. Keough, Donald R. 1996. The challenges of leadership in the next millennium: Ten observations on leadership. Address given to the Hart Leadership Program Distinguished Lecture Series, Duke University, February 13.
7. Interview with author.
8. Elkin, Tobi. 1999. HP unifies branding with $200 million push. *Advertising Age*, **70**(48): 18, November 22.
9. Kehoe, Louise. 1999. Reinventing company of inventors. *Financial Times*, November 16, p. 35.
10. Girl Scout History. www.girlscouts.org.
11. Interview with author.
12. Interview with author.
13. Interview with author.
14. Howard, Robert. 1990. Values make the company: An interview with Robert Haas. *Harvard Business Review*, September–October, pp. 134–43, pp. 135–6.
15. Meyer, Marshall W. and Zucker, Lynne G. 1989. *Permanently Failing Organizations*. Newbury Park, CA: Sage. p. 19.

CHAPTER 5

The Transformer

When Steve Jobs returned to Apple in summer 1997, Apple was facing serious problems, and had undoubtedly lost its way. Market share had dropped precipitously to around 3%, revenue was down 36% over the preceding two years, and the company was on track to lose over $1 billion for the year. Jobs was being brought back to the company he founded to turn around this pioneering company and recapture the glory days of the rebel upstart in the computer industry. He needed to recapture the spirit and vision of the original Apple, to renew the focus of Apple as the creative underdog in an industry filled with "me too's." Within weeks of rejoining the embattled Apple, Jobs launched a compelling advertising campaign that captured what Apple had lost. The campaign featured black and white images of famous pioneers from many fields: Albert Einstein, Pablo Picasso, Martin Luther King, Richard Branson, John Lennon, Mohammed Ali, Ted Turner, Gandhi and many others. As images of these pioneers flashed across the screen, a hopeful, respectful voice toasted these pioneers:

Here's to the crazy ones. The misfits. The rebels. The troublemakers. The round pegs in the square holes. The ones who see things differently. They're not fond of rules, and they have no respect for the status quo. You can quote them, disagree with them, glorify or vilify them. About the only thing you can't do is ignore them. Because they change things. They push the human race forward. And while some may see them as the crazy ones, we see genius. Because the people who are crazy enough to think they can change the world are the ones who do.

In one 60-second commercial, Steve Jobs captured what he was there at Apple to do. Jobs, having been the original Creator of Apple, was essentially there to re-create Apple. This is the role of the Transformer. In many respects, the role of the Transformer is similar to that of the Creator, which is why it is not inconceivable that someone who is essentially a Creator, such as Steve Jobs, can also excel as a Transformer. However, the Transformer's task is made more complicated because the task is one of re-creation from an existing and declining base, rather than starting from scratch as the Creator does. This poses different challenges for the Transformer than those facing the Creator, as the Transformer essentially has two, sometimes conflicting tasks of building and cutting at the same time, in order to halt the decline of the organization and redefine the heroic mission.

Club Méditerranée, or simply Club Med, the French vacation company, begun as a Majorcan tent village in 1950 with an "all-inclusive travel" formula whereby the guests could freely opt in or out of the many activities for an all-inclusive price. Guests, or *gentil membres* (GMs), were hosted by congenial *gentil organisateurs* (GOs) who worked to create a sense of community among the guests and ensure that the guests enjoyed their membership in the village. The concept became a great success, and gained a reputation, particularly among young single vacationers for its *bouffer, bronzer et baiser* (eat, tan, and make love) culture which developed from the free-flowing entertainments of the villages. However, in a classic case, the strengths of Club Med taken to excess began to sow the seeds of decline. While the GOs focused on exuberant celebrations and endless parties in the villages, the cost of these entertainments spiraled out of control. This left less resources available for investment in upkeep and infrastructure of the resorts and they began to look tatty and tired. The number of sports and activities blossomed, requiring experts in each, escalating staff costs. These internal failures, combined with changing external conditions as consumer tastes changed as the baby-boom generation began settling down and having families and the growing fear of AIDS tempered singles' hedonism, resulted in declining attendance in the 1990s, after having reached a peak in 1989–90. Despite an attempt to refocus on the more family-centered vacation market, by this time its competitors had copied the Club Med concept and taken it into the family genre, and Club Med's image, which had made it a household name, was so ingrained that it was a substantial barrier to entice families to its resorts. As a result, Club Med went into a decline through the 1990s and losses mounted to $130 million in 1995–96 and $215 million in 1996–97. However, in February 1997, after a shareholder revolt, Club Med brought in a new chairman, Philippe Bourguignon, who had previously brought Disneyland Paris, or

EuroDisney as it was then known, into profitability. Bourguignon assessed the situation as:

> Club Med is a well-known product but with a fuzzy identity. It is far too French in an international context. We need a complete re-creation of the group. The concept is not outdated, but the image is stuck in the 1970s.[1]

This statement emphasizes the re-creation role of the transformer and the need to restore a sense of vision to the organization that is consistent with its past, but adapted to its current environment. Bourguignon also recognized how the Club Med culture had moved from a strength to a weakness as hubris had crept into the organization:

> All companies have strengths that are weaknesses if you take them too far. The Club's strengths are its unique formula, whereby GOs eat, sport, create shows, and dance with the GMs. [The Club] offers a vast variety of sports, some 60 in total, which we keep extending. We are the largest sports institute in the world. We are located in some of the loveliest places, and our miniclubs for kids are a great success, as is our cuisine. This triangle of GO, GM and site in an atmosphere of generosity and living together needed to be reassessed and rebuilt in an affordable way ... but all these were also expensive and came at the cost of other luxuries and attentions, at higher-than-necessary prices.[2]

Bourguignon set about transforming Club Med with a four-part focus which he termed *Être-Re* or Renew. The four elements of his strategy were: *refocus* – getting the product back on track by renovating the villages; *restore* – rebuilding the reputation of the brand and the product as an all-inclusive vacation; *regain* – closely measuring and evaluating expenses to regain price competitiveness and profitability; *rationalize* – trim management and reorganize, pushing down responsibilities to each village, but retaining the common core that makes each a Club Med vacation.

At the general level, these four strategic elements represent the two major areas of focus for most Transformers: restoring the vision of the organization, and replacing systems which no longer serve the organization well. The first two elements of Bourguignon's strategy really comprise his efforts to re-create the vision for the organization by getting back to the basics of what the initial vision for Club Med was, to provide all-inclusive vacation packages in top-notch resorts. The second two elements represent the efforts to get the organization's systems back on track, rationalizing the organization and establishing new measurement systems to monitor the performance of the organization.

By implementing this four-pronged strategic approach, Philippe Bourguignon was able to turn around the ailing fortunes of Club Med. By 1999, occupancy rates had recovered to 73.5% from 66.9% in 1996. Losses of $130 million in 1996 and $215 million in 1997 turned to profits of $39 million in 1999 and $55 million in 2000.

The Transformer's Organization

Transformers can come into a declining organization that is in essentially one of two states; either the organization recognizes that it is in decline and needs saving or it is in denial and doesn't recognize, and indeed resists, transformational change. If the organization recognizes its need for change, the Transformer comes in with a definite mandate to make the change happen and the organization is generally willing to accept the changes that take place. As such the Transformer can focus on the tasks of fixing the broken systems of the organization and bringing in a new vision for the organization's future. However, even when the organization as a whole knows that it is in need of renewal, there can be departments or divisions of the company that are performing better than the overall organization and do not themselves feel the same need for change. One of the most well-known Transformers of recent years, "Chainsaw Al," Albert Dunlap took the helm of Scott Paper in April 1994, the company having lost $277 million the previous year. While the company certainly recognized the financial trouble it was in, Dunlap recounted that, "the deepest trouble came because Scott's management and employees no longer believed the company's decline could be stopped."[3] However, even though the company overall was in deep decline, there were divisions that were performing fairly well who questioned the need for changes in their divisions. Dunlap remarked:[4]

> I was not the cause of the average Scott employee's discomfort in 1994. I was the result of the previous administration's having created a train wreck out of a once successful company. But people within the company had difficulty accepting that fact, particularly those in what were the company's pockets of excellence and competence.

> Everything was not bad. Scott had some terrific people and some great business units, such as the European Consumer and Away-From-Home Worldwide divisions; the latter developed and marketed commercial and industrial cleaning products. Many of those people couldn't understand why everyone had to

endure the pain and torture of restructuring. The answer was that we had to become competitive across the board, not just in one division. We had to be efficient and unload a lot of the rubbish that years of poor management had heaped on itself.

Thus while resistance to change can be an issue even when the company sees the urgency of its decline, this is compounded when the organization is in denial about the need for drastic change. In such cases, the major task that faces the Transformer is the need to convey a sense of urgency to the organization. Many organizations fail to recognize that they are in decline and in need of a turnaround at all. After many years of sustained success, the signs of a slow descent can be easy to miss for those inside the organization who do not perceive that things are getting slightly worse all the time. It is relatively easy to explain a small percentage drop in revenues or profits as being affected by one-time events or unusual circumstances or a short-term downturn. Indeed, it is this very myopia which usually implies that a Transformer needs to come from outside the organization – not just as a source of fresh ideas, but to actually see the trouble the company is in. Sometimes, particularly in closely held private companies, or divisions of larger companies where seemingly limitless resources are provided by the parent company, the dire nature of the situation may well be deliberately hidden from even the senior managers. Marilyn Marks purchased Dorsey Trailers, a manufacturer of trailers for the trucking industry based in the southeastern United States, which had been under private family control, and then held as a division of a much larger corporate entity who kept covering the losses of the Dorsey division:

> What happened was because the company had been on such a nice growth trend for so long, the expectations of the employees was so high. When the business flattened out and began to decline, management, with the paternalistic attitude they had always had with employees, treated them as if times were better than they were. As it turns out about this story, many of the accumulated profits and retained earnings were given to the employees as yearly bonuses and employees never knew the company was continuing to lose money. They were given bonuses and life was going on as if it was a competitive, well-run organization. ... When I bought it, it had been run for decades in such a way that not even the senior managers were aware of the profitability of the company. Much less the hourly employees. And I remember sharing the financials of the company with the vice presidents. They had only been shown financial information or data from their areas, and only a few people had seen data from the company overall. The senior managers did not have a realistic

picture of how the company fit into the industry, or how it fit into the parent company. Therefore, I tried to promote a culture of "everyone needs to know how we're doing, whether it's good or bad." That sounded so easy. But it was so difficult because these senior managers who were in their fifties or sixties had just for the first time seen these numbers. And this had been such treasured data that they didn't want to share it.[5]

In such an environment, it is difficult even conveying the sense of urgency and crisis that is needed to stimulate the change necessary for a turnaround.

Even when a change in the external environment is recognized, the danger it poses to the company often is not, as the organization falls back on what it does well, believing that the environment will return to the conditions that enabled the company to prosper in former times. When Marilyn Marks took over Dorsey Trailers, it was at a point in time when the regulatory environment facing the company had recently changed. The Surface Transportation Act of 1982 had deregulated the industry of its customers, so that whereas the trucking companies that Dorsey supplied had previously not been too concerned with the costs of the product, as they passed them on to their customers, and had focused on the quality of the product and reputation of the brand, both of which Dorsey was known for, now cost became the primary focus. However, Dorsey had not responded to this change, retaining its focus on the quality of its product without regard to cost. Marks recalled:

I'll never forget my first meeting with senior managers in the company right after the purchase. One of the stronger, more vocal members of senior management said, "Marilyn, don't come in here trying to have a lot of new ideas of how you are going to deal with trucking deregulation. Because trucking regulation is going to come back; all we need to do is hold on, do exactly what we are doing, and eventually trucking will be re-regulated and we will be in the perfect place." While the general population of the factory had no idea about trucking deregulation, that statement probably spoke volumes about the culture there at the factory: "Don't change anything, let us operate the way we have been operating."[6]

This resistance to change based on the naive belief that things will get better by themselves, even in less blatant examples than this, is often a strong barrier for the Transformer to overcome in order to enact change in the organization.

The Transformer's Task

The Transformer's task is essentially twofold: to halt the decline of the organization and instill a renewed sense of vision into the organization in order to revitalize it and enable it to grow once again. Marilyn Marks characterizes the emphasis a Transformer needs to place on these two tasks as a distinction between financially driven and culturally driven turnarounds:

> I would begin to make a distinction in the types of turnarounds. Sometimes turnarounds are much more financially driven and I think those take a different type of leader than those that are culturally driven. In our case we had both, but I can tell you from experience that the financial part is so much easier than the cultural world. For example, when I bought the company, the average days payable was six days, average days receivables was 126 days. It was not a matter of bad debts; the company had an excellent bad debt experience with very little bad debts. It was just that since funding had never been an issue, why not let your customers have that long to pay, and pay your vendors fast? You get popular that way. Certainly it's not easy to get your customers to go from paying in 120 days to a floor-plan arrangement where they paid us the minute the trailer was built. That was a massive change for them, but it turned out to have a massive financial impact as well. And we reversed the situation on the payables as well. You have to deal with a lot of people – vendors, customers, banks, salesmen who have to sell this. But changing those types of financial levers, in theory, is not nearly as difficult as leading a group of people on how the basic operation of the business has to change. That's why I'm suggesting to you that you will have different leaders who can do those different jobs. On the financial side, there will be people who will be much more hard-nosed who will say from their corner office, "we are doing it this way … " and still have a financial turnaround to their credit. The much more difficult aspect was the cultural one.[7]

Here Marks equates halting the decline of the organization with tightening the financial controls needed in the organization and renewing the vision with changing the ingrained culture of the organization. However, as Marks indicates in her own situation, often these two tasks are intertwined and less separable than would at first appear in a turnaround. So while in some turnarounds, a Transformer may have a strong second in command, typically a chief financial officer, who takes the lead on internal controls, more typically the Transformer him- or herself will unify both roles, as although the financial controls and culture change seem like separate activities, decisions in one area have an impact on the other.

When Carlos Ghosn took over the leadership of Nissan, Nissan's market share in its home market, Japan, had been eroding for over 25 years; having reached a peak of 33.7% in 1972, it was down to 17.8% in 2000. The company was stumbling beneath a huge $17 billion debt burden and its cars were considered unexciting at best and deadly boring at worst. In March 1999, Renault, seeing the need to join forces with an international partner to compete with the likes of DaimlerChrysler, purchased 36.8% of Nissan and installed Ghosn, a Brazilian native of Lebanese descent who had worked for Renault in France since 1996, to turn Nissan around.

One of the keys for a successful turnaround for a Transformer is the ability to question everything, to leave no process, relationship, or routine sacred in revitalizing the organization. It is primarily for this reason that successful Transformers almost always come from outside the organization, as they have no loyalty or prior commitment to any aspect of the status quo which might hinder change within the organization. For Ghosn, this was a formidable challenge, given the strong *keiretsu* (business group) relationships Nissan had with suppliers and banks that went back decades, cemented by cross-ownership ties as well as commercial relationships. Going against a strong cultural norm, both for the company itself, and for Japanese industry generally, Ghosn demanded that Nissan placed orders with suppliers without regard to their previous *keiretsu* relationships, but based on global price competitiveness. By March 2002, purchasing costs were cut by 18%, using 35% fewer vendors. Ghosn also went against ingrained cultural norms by closing some plants in Japan, while spending $1 billion to triple capacity at its engine factory in Tennessee and building a plant in Mississippi, focusing on producing vehicles as close as possible to the markets where they are sold. As a result, production at domestic Japanese plants rose from 51% of capacity before Ghosn took over to 76% by the end of 2001 against a benchmark of 70%, generally regarded as the breakeven point for automobile plants. In the year to March 2001, the second year under Ghosn, Nissan posted a profit of $2.7 billion; its first annual profit in four years, and the largest profit in the company's 68-year history.[8]

When organizations are in decline and financial measures have spiraled out of control, the Transformer needs to set a demarcation point and set dramatic targets to demonstrate both the urgency and drastic nature of the changes required to get the organization back on course. In 1991 Michael Kay became CEO of LSG/SKY Chefs, a company that provides catering services to airlines, where costs had begun to escalate and profitability was declining. Kay set about the role of the Transformer and, over three years, reduced operating costs by \$60 million and more than doubled operating profits. In recording the lessons for Transformers, Kay wrote:

> The CEO has to produce results fast or the whole enterprise will go up in smoke. So the first order of business is to understand the bare bones of the company and, in consultation with key managers, to set turnaround objectives – for the company, for decentralized units, for processes, and for individual managers. These value objectives, or targets, should be tightly focused and detailed. But, above all, they should be breathtakingly bold – the most ambitious bogeys possible. Avoid thinking in terms of small steps and reasonable increments like a 10 to 15 percent improvement for this or that function or operation … Incremental gains have no place in a turnaround. What you must demand is major transformation fueled by explosive and revolutionary ideas.[9]

Speed in instituting action is thus essential for the Transformer. Not only is this necessary due to the ailing condition of the organization, but also to prompt the sense of urgency in the organization necessary for a successful turnaround. Incoming Transformers will often make bold, visible moves as soon as possible after taking office in order to symbolize the need for change and that the Transformer is prepared to take the organization through drastic, wrenching change. However, it is important that the Transformer also paints a picture of what life will be like on the other side of the transformation of the organization to give employees the motivation and vision that the pain is worth enduring. This is essentially the second task of the Transformer, to re-create the vision for the organization, and is intertwined with the first task of rationalizing the organization's operations.

Often the re-creation of the vision is not so much installing a completely new vision for the organization as it is returning the organization that has lost its way to its original vision. Archie Norman took over as CEO of the Asda supermarket chain in the UK in 1991. At the time Asda had been declining, dropping to a poor fourth place in food retailing behind Tesco, Sainsbury's and Safeway. Fundamentally, though, Asda had lost its way as it tried to compete with Sainsbury's and Tesco by moving upmarket, using a prominent designer to remodel the stores, widening their range, adding own-label products and new layers of management to support the stores. In doing so, however, Asda's costs rose, forcing up prices and moving Asda away from its core customers – three-quarters of Asda stores were in areas where the population earned average and below-average incomes – who focused on the cheapest price in their food purchases. Asda had also branched out through acquisition into other non-food retailing such as furniture and carpets, which had led to a £1 billion debt burden, the servicing of which was crippling the company. Archie Norman's challenge was to return Asda to its original mission, which he termed the "Virtuous Circle," restoring the traditional Asda price differential of 5–7% below its competitors and helpful, friendly service. While this was certainly enabled by financial maneuverings, such as selling off the peripheral businesses, selling some property, ceasing speculative property development, and raising funds through a rights issue, the core of the transformation was cultural, refocusing the vision of the organization around the "Asda Way of Working."[10]

This new approach was designed to transform what had become an autocratic and slow moving culture to one where employees enjoyed working and would consequently provide customer service "with a personality derived from the heart of the company." To do this, Norman took a number of small, but interlocked measures which cumulatively had a profound effect on the overall culture. These ranged from introducing share options to all employees on the same terms as top executives, allowing everyone to feel a real sense of ownership in what they were doing, to improving communication through twice daily "huddles" between managers and their teams in the stores rather than weekly managers' meetings. Symbolism abounded to visibly demonstrate the new attitude. The one reserved parking spot at headquarters was for the company Jaguar, but it was not driven by Norman, but by the winner of the monthly competition for the employee – colleagues as they are known at Asda – whose efforts brought about the biggest increase in sales of a particular item. All the offices were open-plan, encouraging the sharing of ideas, although if sustained thinking was required, people could signal their desire to not be disturbed by wearing an Asda baseball cap. Meeting rooms were plentiful, but without chairs to encourage short, to-the-point meetings. A "Tell Archie" suggestion scheme allowing colleagues to put suggestions directly to Norman attracted 14,000 suggestions in the first 18 months and these were rewarded by everything from pens to trips to Paris. Decision-making was pushed down to enable teams to run departments under the ethos of running their own market stalls within the store, as teams had their own accountability for the profitability of their department. Senior management cultivated an atmosphere of approachability and teams were expected to challenge management decisions if appropriate and make decisions on their own. All these changes, while individually small, collectively culminated in a tangible change in the culture and atmosphere of the stores and focused the organization back onto its core customer and the original vision for the organization of providing choice and friendly service at a price a little below what other supermarkets charged. The changes also transformed the bottom line for Asda, with profits leaping from £168.3 million in 1991 to £304 million in 1996 when Norman turned over the CEO role to Allan Leighton.

The task of the Transformer then is to essentially draw the proverbial line in the sand, marking a changing point for the organization, setting targets, and painting the vision of the future. In order to accomplish a successful turnaround, the Transformer normally needs to effect change quickly, making the dramatic and often painful changes in one short swoop, so that the pain of the turnaround is not prolonged and employees do not become disillusioned by not knowing whether or not they are part of the organization's future. As Al Dunlap stated:

> I believe that, when you go into a situation like this, you either get the pain and suffering accomplished in the first twelve months or you don't do it at all. There are no three-year restructuring plans in my line of work. If a restructuring is done over three years, moods and corporate directions change. The longer it takes, the greater the opportunity for the old corporate culture to corrupt it.[11]

The Transformer needs to ensure early visible successes and milestones of progress towards the transformation of the organization and consequently should pick the low hanging fruit of the organization – those easily identifiable and fixable changes which make a noticeable difference to the operations of the organization. The Transformer also has to be aware of the symbolism that comes from making changes and use this symbolism to his or her advantage, demonstrating the progress that is being made and using symbols to mold the new culture of the organization. Indeed, using symbols to get across the message of impending change and a new or refocused mission for the organization is critical from the first day a Transformer takes over an organization. Ron Sargent, CEO of office supply chain Staples Inc., used his first day in just such a manner:

> On my first day as CEO, I put on the black pants, black shoes, and red shirt that our associates wear and headed to our Brighton store. We opened the very first Staples store in Brighton, Massachusetts in 1986, and by going there, I tried to rally the Staples troops around a concept that I call "Back to Brighton." It's a symbolic message to the members of our organization that we're going to improve service and refocus on our core customer base: the small-business customer.[12]

The Transformer's Leadership Style

The tasks of dispassionate analysis and drastically changing a company's operations, together with putting a new vision in place could imply that the Transformer needs to encompass a wide range of styles. Indeed, Transformers need perhaps the greatest variety of skills and qualities of any of the leadership roles. They need to be both detail oriented, able to focus on the key variables in restoring the company's systems, and big picture oriented, able to paint a future vision past the immediate pain that lies ahead. They need to be hands on enough to grasp the details and ensure that the transformation is taking place, but delegate enough so that subordinates and teams are empowered to enact the transformational change.

Michael Kay at LSG/SKY Chefs believes that although the Transformer sets the agenda and pushes the organization to achieve radical goals that it would not set for itself, the results are achieved by teams, and so the Transformer's style needs to be more like a coach, encouraging his or her team while holding them to account for their performance:

> CEOs must lead without claiming to have any magic bullets. They should inspire, motivate, and sometimes astonish middle managers who truly do have the details of the business in their grasp. The bullets they have to keep dodging are people coming to them for answers. The leadership style of successful CEOs depends on delegating authority to the special-purpose teams they create, alter, and dissolve as the turnaround progresses. Much of their effort has to be dedicated to exhorting middle managers to believe in the culture change they're sponsoring. They must encourage their managers to trust the new values of high goals, high performance, and constant accountability – blending a bottom-line focus with an astute perception of what it takes to motivate people to surpass themselves.

> At SKY Chefs, I have focused on special-purpose teams because experience showed that they have the capacity to achieve rapid and dramatic operating improvements. But teams are equally important as the company's model of governance. Once our teams demonstrated their capabilities, everyone in management realized that this was a superior tool for managing the day-to-day business. The team approach promised to retain and extend our hard-won operating gains because constant improvements and refinements would clearly be necessary to sustain top performance. In the final analysis, teams are more than organizational structures. They represent a superior behavioral style – a

way of tackling challenges large and small that virtually guarantee a company's capacity to respond to the demands of change and to command its own future.[13]

Most importantly, Transformers, as is true for leaders in all the roles, need to lead by example. Turnarounds take a lot of work and consequently a preparedness to put in the required effort. Carlos Ghosn picked up the nickname "7–11" at Nissan for the long hours he keeps. Before that, at Renault, he was known as "le cost killer" for his tenacity at reducing excess costs in the system. Often turnarounds represent hardships and the need for everyone to be prepared to make sacrifices to ensure the survival of the organization. Successful Transformers exemplify this sacrificial behavior by visibly putting their own welfare on the line or making symbolic sacrifices themselves. For example, when Steve Jobs returned to Apple, just as Lee Iacocca had done years before at Chrysler, he took a salary of just $1 per year to symbolize the drastic nature of what needed to be done. One of the more unusual examples is John Lauer, who in 1997 took over as CEO of Oglebay-Norton, an industrial minerals and shipping company in Cleveland, Ohio. Lauer, who at the time was writing a doctoral thesis on executive compensation, refused to be paid a salary, but took "premium" options, with an exercise price 25% higher than the market price at the time, which, if exercised, would give him 8% of the company. He also invested over $1 million of his own money, buying Oglebay-Norton shares on the open market. Thus, Lauer left himself in the position where he needed to raise the price of the stock by over a quarter to earn anything for his job, and was subject to diminishing wealth if the stock price went down. His philosophy on CEO compensation is that the leader needs to be seen to be taking the greatest risk if he or she is to lead others in a turnaround, and the leader should not benefit if the turnaround is unsuccessful, but the rewards for success need to be there as well. He comments:

> My payday, if I succeed, will be very large: an option to buy 8% of Oglebay Norton. My ethic is that if you are willing to take the risk and put your money up there and work hard, it is OK if you get paid really well. But it is structured in a way that is not a low-risk or no-risk approach to CEO compensation.[14]

As to the effect such a package has on the motivation of others in the organization, Lauer is confident that the risk he is taking provides impetus for others:

You are investing in yourself, the confidence you have in your own abilities to succeed and perform under certain measurements. Employees recognize that.

It creates a much more interesting dynamic, that "Wow, here's a guy who came into the company [and] invested his own money. If he wins, we are all going to win. I would rather work for a guy like that, than somebody maybe who is motivated differently."

That attitude has made a difference in the type of person we attract into management. And it makes a difference in how people relate to management. I receive e-mails from all over the company and letters from retirees that they really like what I did.[15]

Transitions from Decline

Where the organization transitions from the Decline phase in the lifecycle it is not necessarily to terminal decline for the organization. If the turn-around performed by the Transformer has been successful, the organization will transition to a period of renewed growth and stability, rejuvenating the organization and recycling through the lifecycle. Indeed, as the organization goes into a period of decline, Transformers can extend the lifecycle of the organization indefinitely by going through multiple turnarounds, such that the lifecycle resembles a bumpy plateau, as shown in Figure 5.1.

However, even in successful turnarounds, when the organization re-enters a new period of growth and stability, it is probable that as the Transformer role returns to one of either Accelerator or Sustainer, there will be a change in the person leading the organization. In this instance, more often than not, this succession occurs because the Transformer feels less engaged in sustaining success and more driven by the challenge of rescuing ailing organizations, and so will go and seek a similar challenge elsewhere having succeeded in turning around the organization. Thus, just as Transformers come in as a "knight in shining armor" to save the company, they will ride off into the sunset to begin another adventure, leaving the organization in the hands of an Accelerator or Sustainer. Archie Norman exemplifies this modus operandi, seeing his role as effecting substantial change in major companies and then moving on:

What I do is business management, leadership and organizational change. My big thing is that I like to make a big difference, a big change. I don't see myself

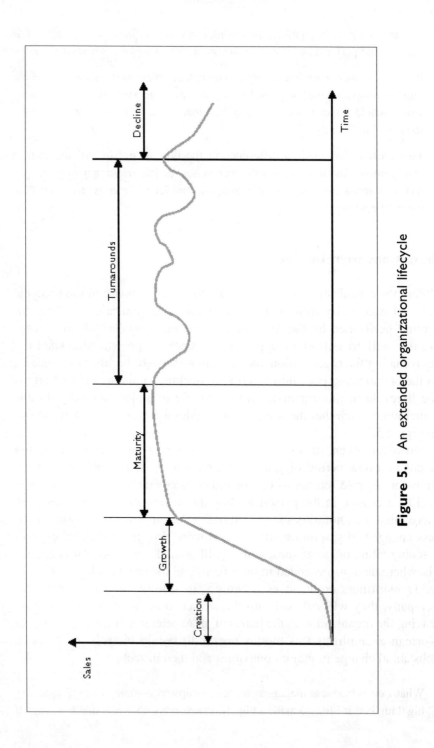

Figure 5.1 An extended organizational lifecycle

as collecting non-executive directorships. I do my best when I bring intense focus and change to a business.[16]

Similarly, Al Dunlap sees his role clearly as a Transformer and is not interested in staying with organizations that he has turned around and taking on the role of a Sustainer:

> The final, recurring criticism of me is that I have never proved myself as a long-term manager, only as a turnaround specialist. Our emphasis at Scott Paper on marketing, developing a global strategy, and building new manufacturing facilities shows we were planning for a long-term future. But there is some truth to this polemic as well. I crave the challenge of a major restructuring. There's nothing better than being handed a ton of clay and assigned to mold and shape it into a beautiful piece of art.
>
> By contrast, when things are going well, where's the challenge in that? Eventually, I have gotten bored every place I have been.
>
> Once a company becomes business-as-usual, it loses its appeal for me. I honestly feel that the infamous Al Dunlap doesn't exist except when confronted with extraordinarily difficult situations. I am entranced by situations where I can make great change, have a major impact, challenge my abilities, and create enormous wealth for shareholders.[17]

However, while organizations that go through a successful turnaround under a Transformer return to the Growth or Maturity phases, organizations do fail and go into terminal decline for one reason or another. A quick glance over the decades of the Fortune 500 shows that even the largest companies can decline and fail, or at least lose their independence through being acquired and folded into another organization. As noted in the opening chapter, one third of the Fortune 500 listed in 1970 had disappeared by 1993, being either acquired, merged, broken into pieces or falling into outright bankruptcy.[18]

As we will see in Chapter 7 which looks at organizations in transition, organizations can go into rapid terminal decline at any of the transition points through the lifecycle. However, large organizations, having progressed through the Maturity phase of the lifecycle, generally fail due to a drastic change in their environment. Such a change either renders their core competence obsolete, in which case the organization either dies completely, or shrinks to a specialist niche producer, or the market change makes their scale inadequate, thus necessitating consolidation within the industry, which means that the firm either acquires others to become a dominant player, or is acquired by someone else.

As large companies grow in the market and go through their Maturity phases, so industries themselves mature and become more stable. Jagdish Sheth and Rajendra Sisodia[19] contend that, as industries mature, a natural market structure develops, allowing three large generalist organizations to exist which between them control 70–90% of the market, with the rest of the market taken by small, niche companies filling specialist gaps in the market left by the generalists. Thus, as the industry matures, along with maturing companies within the industry, consolidation occurs as the industry moves towards this natural market structure. For the individual company, the time comes when it realizes that it cannot compete in its maturing industry at its present scale and the company must determine whether it has the will and the resources to acquire others to achieve sufficient scale, or whether to position itself to be acquired by someone with such an ambition. If the latter, the strategic objective switches to realizing the maximum value possible for the company. However, once the end of an independent existence becomes apparent to the organization, uncertainty increases dramatically, particularly for the employees of the company, and the challenge for the Terminator lies in keeping the organization focused and functioning in order to maximize the value of the organization.

Notes

1. Jack, Andrew, 1998. Club Med Chairman details shake-up. *Financial Times*, January 28.
2. Trompenaars, Frons, and Hampden-Turner, Charles. 2001. *21 Leaders for the 21st Century: How Innovative Leaders Manage in the Digital Age*. Oxford: Capstone Publishing, p. 113.
3. Dunlap, Albert J. with Andelman, Bob, 1996. *Mean Business: How I Save Bad Companies and Make Good Companies Great*. New York: Times Books, p. x.
4. Ibid, p. 9.
5. Interview with author.
6. Interview with author.
7. Interview with author.
8. Raskin, Andy. 2002. Voulez-vous completely overhaul this big, slow company and start making some cars people actually want avec moi? *Business*, 2.0 January, pp. 60–7.
9. Kay, Michael Z. 1998. Memo to a turnaround boss. In Dauphinais, G. William, and Price, Colin, (eds) *Straight from the CEO: The World's Top Business Leaders Reveal Ideas that Every Manager Can Use*. New York: Simon & Schuster, pp. 149, 151.
10. van deVliet, Anita. 1995. Asda's open plan. *Management Today*, December, pp. 50–4.
11. See note 3, pp. 11–12.
12. Overholt, Alison. 2002. New Leaders, New Agenda. *Fast Company*, May, pp. 52–62, p. 60.
13. See note 9, pp. 154–5.

14. Lublin, Joann S. 2001. Investing in himself: CEO John Lauer talks about why he chose to get paid only if he performs – and why so few others take the same risk. *Wall Street Journal*, April 12.
15. Ibid.
16. Rankine, Kate. 2002. Norman plans FTSE comeback. *Daily Telegraph*, February 25.
17. See note 3, p. 26.
18. de Geus, Arie. 1997. *The Living Company: Habits for Survival in a Turbulent Business Environment*. Boston, MA: Harvard Business School Press.
19. Sheth, Jagdish, and Sisodia, Rajendra. 2002. *The Rule of Three: Why Only Three Major Competitors will Survive in Any Market*. New York: Free Press.

CHAPTER 6

The Terminator

Terminators bring closure to an organization. However, this does not necessarily imply the failure of the organization, nor a leadership failure. Organizations can indeed fail, as we will explore further in the next chapter, by not effectively transitioning from one lifestage to the next, resulting in a mismatch between the lifestage of the organization and the particular role being played by the leader. Organizations can also fail because of a failure of leadership in any of the organizational lifestages, either by the ineffective fulfillment of the leadership role that matches the organization's lifestage or by following an inappropriate leadership role for the current lifestage. However, there are circumstances where organizations reach the end of their existence, or at least their independence as a stand-alone organization, which do not represent failure. This can be because of either the fulfillment of the organization's objectives or the strategic decision or realization that the organization is best served by being a part of a larger organization. In either of these cases, there is the need for a leadership role that takes the organization through this critical transition.

The Terminator role thus occurs primarily in two circumstances: when an organization's mission is fulfilled, often being temporary from the outset, and winds up; or when an organization loses its independence by being acquired by another organization. In the latter case, the Terminator role does not represent the final leadership role in the organization, but rather a transitional role as the organization loses its independence and is merged into another organization. In such a case, the organization will often emerge as a division of another company where a leadership role appropriate to the status of the division in its lifecycle within the larger organization will become appropriate.

The Terminator in Temporary Organizations

Temporary organizations are those that are designed to be temporary from the moment they are created. For suborganizations within organizations this is common, with ad hoc project teams being formed and disbanded as projects come and go. In such cases, the larger organization continues, and those people who have been involved in a particular project move to other projects or groups within the organization. However, there are whole organizations which are set up specifically as temporary organizations, and while leaders of temporary groups within larger organizations face some of the same challenges, these are exaggerated for leaders of temporary organizations. Movie-making and large sporting events are good examples. In making a movie, a sizable, temporary organization is set up including actors, the director, producers, stuntmen, set designers and builders, and a plethora of support crews. The end credits to any major movie usually encompass several hundred people, all of whom come together for the specific purpose of making the movie and then disband again after the movie is completed. Some may work together again on other movies, but the entire organization is not directly reassembled. Similarly, a major sporting event, such as the Olympic Games, requires a temporary organization of enormous magnitude. The 1996 Olympic Games in Atlanta, for example, constituted the largest peacetime event in world history, bigger than the 1984 Olympic Games in Los Angeles and the 1992 Olympic Games in Barcelona combined.

On February 8, 1987, Billy Payne, an Atlanta lawyer, had the idea to bring the Olympics to his home city. Despite no government backing, skepticism from the local community, and little initial support from the business community, Payne persisted and slowly built support, and on September 18, 1990, the International Olympic Committee awarded the Games to Atlanta. The Atlanta Committee for the Olympic Games (ACOG) was the temporary organization then formed to put on the Games. In March 1991, A.D. Frazier, an Atlanta bank executive, was hired as Chief Operating Officer to run the ACOG with Payne. By mid-1992, there were 200 full-time paid staff and, by March 1994, there were 1600. By the time the Games took place in July 1996, the total operation involved 4,000 employees, 57,000 contractors, 1,900 staff loaned from sponsoring organizations, and 47,600 volunteers. Three months after the games, only a small skeleton staff remained in order to dispose of the assets of the organization and close the books, and by the next summer the organization had completely vanished. In the space of six years, a Fortune 500-sized company had been created and disbanded.

Such temporary organizations create unique challenges for leaders who run them, especially as the end of the organization draws near. For one thing, the realization that the organization is drawing to a close can often produce separation anxiety in the people who have been deeply involved in the organization. Although true in many temporary organizations where people have identified with the goals of the organization, this is exaggerated in the extreme in an organization such as the ACOG which people realize will be the most significant event or organization that they will ever be a part of. As Billy Payne said in the months following the 1996 Olympics:

> Nothing I'll ever do will have the same level of public profile, the same stress, the same kind of critical deadlines, and the same enormity as what I've just done. But if my next endeavors aren't as big because they can't be, I've made peace with that.[1]

Part of the leader's challenge, therefore, is to help others in the organization to make peace with the forthcoming disbandment of the organization. A counterbalancing part of the impending separation anxiety that may be felt by members of the organization is a sense of meaninglessness in their work once the main goals have been accomplished, and the subsequent lack of motivation for the work and desire to move on, particularly as others leave the organization. Following the closing ceremonies of the Games on August 4, 1996, and even before, as employees began to sense that their task was accomplished, the leadership challenge became one of maintaining motivation in key people who were needed to bring closure to the organization, such that the satisfaction that they had felt in accomplishing this enormous task of putting on the Games wasn't undermined by failing to attend effectively to tying up the loose ends after the Games themselves were over.

Part of the Terminator's task lies in managing the winding-down process by dealing with the practical dimensions of closing. In the case of the ACOG, for the first time in Olympic history, they offered outplacement services to both athletes and staff to ease the transition. However, in addition to the management processes that can ease the practicalities of the transition, such as outplacement and severance packages, Terminators need to manage the emotional dimension of the organization. Part of achieving this comes from the legacy that the organization leaves behind and can come in the form of a remaining symbolic presence. In the ACOG's case, the leaving of the Olympic cauldron that held the flame next to the Olympic stadium, and Centennial Olympic Park, complete with

Olympic-ring fountains in the heart of downtown Atlanta, left permanent symbols of the legacy of the ACOG's existence.

The Terminator in Acquired Organizations

Sometimes organizations cannot survive as independent entities, or would be more effective competitively as part of a larger organization. This can be due, for example, to the consolidation of an industry which forces competitors to merge in order to gain the benefits of scale economies. While some companies may be forced into being acquired at the natural end of their lifecycle, having descended into a period of decline, acquisition can be a strategic decision by the organization and can occur at any point in the lifecycle. For example, it happens not infrequently to smaller companies who, due to their limited size and reach, do not have the resources, be they financial, manufacturing or distribution, to realize their potential and so take the strategic decision to be acquired by a larger organization in order to gain access to the relevant resources. Thus, some organizations may be acquired in or between their Creation and Growth phases in order to facilitate growth which they would be unable to achieve as an independent entity. This is especially true when the company requires rapid growth beyond what could be achieved through internal growth, for example because of a very short product lifecycle and the consequent small market window where the product is likely to be successful. Thus, even though the company is moving from the Creation to Growth phase, its movement between these phases by being acquired requires the brief leadership role of a Terminator in order to successfully make this transition. A good example of this is Palm Computing, makers of the Palm Pilot.

Palm Computing was founded by Jeff Hawkins, who believed that there was a market for handheld computers which performed limited, but useful, functions.[2] In 1991, as head of research for a company called GRiD Systems, he had pioneered a pen-based computer, the GRiDPad, which was marketed for professional applications such as by insurance claims adjusters or meter readers. Although it was somewhat bulky and expensive, thus restricting its uses to the professional arena, Hawkins was confident of a large market for simpler, smaller, and cheaper machines aimed at the general public. GRiD, however, wasn't interested in the consumer market, so Hawkins tried to interest GRiD's corporate parent, Tandy Corporation, known for their Radio Shack stores, in the idea. Tandy was indeed very interested and asked Hawkins to head the development of this device, which he named Zoomer. Hawkins, however, was not convinced that he could attract the right engineers to build the device within the corporate umbrella of Tandy, and preferred to strike out on his own. Although Tandy was initially not happy about this, eventually a deal was worked out where Tandy invested $300,000 into Hawkins' company, and with an additional $1 million in venture capital, Hawkins launched Palm Computing on January 2, 1992. He immediately hired some software engineers to help him, and very shortly thereafter a CEO, Donna Dubinsky, formerly of Apple Computer, who could lead the company as Hawkins led the product development effort.

Tandy also brought other partners to the table, and the Zoomer quickly became a collaborative effort with Casio, a Japanese manufacturer of calculators, watches and other consumer electronics, who would manufacture the device and sell it under the Casio name, and GeoWorks, who had an operating system for handheld devices. The device would then be sold primarily through Tandy's Radio Shack stores. However, far from easing the process, the collaboration quickly led to conflict between the four main parties involved with Palm, and Hawkins began losing control of what the device would look like and which features it would contain, with Casio quickly becoming the dominant partner. Meanwhile, competition in the new market for personal digital assistants (PDAs), a term coined by John Sculley of Apple Computer, was heating up. Apple was preparing to launch its own PDA, the Newton, which also featured handwriting recognition and many more features than Palm had planned for the Zoomer. Additionally, Apple, an established company well known for innovative products and its marketing prowess, was also garnering the lion's share of media attention for the Newton. However, Apple, having publicized the Newton back in 1992, and continually hyping the product since then, despite continually pushing back the launch date, finally released the Newton in August 1993. Although Apple instantly sold all 40,000 Newtons it had produced for the launch, within a few weeks the Newton had turned into a public relations nightmare for Apple, as complaints rolled in about how cumbersome it was and how poor the handwriting recognition was. Sales of the Newton dropped off dramatically. While on the one hand, the failure of the Newton might have been good news for Palm, in fact, the hype that the Newton had generated, and its subsequent failure to live up to the expectations that consumers now had for these new PDAs, meant that public perception turned against the devices. Thus, when the Zoomer hit stores in early October, although it ratcheted up

20,000 sales in the first two months during the peak holiday season, by the new year, sales had slowed dramatically.

Meanwhile, before the Zoomer had even hit the stores, Palm was already working on the next generation Zoomer II, which would be smaller, faster, and simpler to use. However, in early 1994, with the slow-down in Zoomer sales, Casio pulled the plug on the Zoomer II. This left Palm with little business and wondering how it would survive. However, in April 1994, in a discussion on its future with one of its venture capital backers, the VC Bruce Dunlevie suggested that if Hawkins and Dubinsky were confident that Hawkins' vision for a simple organizer device would be a big hit with a wider consumer audience, Palm itself should pursue that vision, and design and manufacture such a device rather than just trying to make application software for other handheld devices from other manufacturers. Despite the conventional wisdom that said that there was more profit to be made in software than hardware, and the higher risk of hardware development, the company had little practical choice if it was to survive as a going concern but to actually make its own device. This change in strategic direction, however, meant that it needed to raise more money, which Dubinsky estimated at $5 million, in order to develop the product and see it through launch.

So while Hawkins set to work on the device, which was code named Touchdown, Dubinsky set off to raise a further $5 million. Unfortunately however, with the failure of the Newton, the Zoomer, and a couple of other high-profile PDAs, the venture capital community was now shying away from handheld devices and was not interested in investing in Palm. Even the three main VC investors who were already backing Palm would not put in any more money unless Palm also secured an investment from a larger company who would also partner with Palm on the product. Dubinsky came close to deals with Motorola, who had supplied the chips for the Zoomer, then Ericsson, the cellular phone company, and finally Compaq, but there were problems with at least two of the deals as Motorola wanted to buy the company to utilize Palm's technology in its own products and Compaq demanded increasingly onerous terms as it realized the weakness of Palm's negotiating position, to the point where the deal became unacceptable to Palm.

While Dubinsky was still negotiating with Ericsson and Compaq, Palm also pitched the idea to a modem manufacturer, U.S. Robotics, whose recently acquired subsidiary, Megahertz, was in negotiations with Palm to build a modem for Touchdown. U.S. Robotics' CEO Casey Cowell, and Jon Zakin, Executive Vice President of Strategy and Business Development, instantly loved Palm's plans and prototype of Touchdown, but

instead of offering an investment in the company, offered to buy the
company outright, seeing a strategic fit with Palm. Dubinsky and Hawkins
didn't want to sell the company, but as the development on Touchdown
was progressing, the need for money was becoming desperate and the
reality was that, without some investment, the company would go under
before Touchdown could be launched. Dubinsky recalled saying to one of
her VC backers who was unsure of selling: "I'd really like not to sell the
company, too. I just don't see how to get around it. Just who is going to
invest in Palm?"[3] So, at the same time as pursuing a deal with Compaq,
Dubinsky also pursued the acquisition by U.S. Robotics. However, even
the impending deal with U.S. Robotics didn't seem to improve Palm's
negotiating position with Compaq, who even tightened up the clauses in
its proposed contract so that it became even less acceptable to Palm. As
Dubinsky put it:

> In the end, the option for us was that we would be a captive supplier for
> Compaq, and they would invest one million dollars. It didn't seem like a good
> deal. The irony was, an acquisition by U.S. Robotics looked more like it would
> grant us independence than the Compaq deal.[4]

Retaining their independence and getting the Touchdown to market were
the two priorities for Hawkins and Dubinsky. Zakin promised that Palm
would be allowed to operate independently and control the design of their
product, but was also persuasive that being part of U.S. Robotics would be
strategically ideal for Palm because of U.S. Robotics' great distribution
network and relationship to retail stores, their well-known brand name
among computer users and the willingness to put the resources necessary
behind the launch of Palm's product. These assurances, backed up by
hearing from its CEO about the positive experiences of Megahertz, which
had been acquired by U.S. Robotics six months previously, convinced
Dubinsky and Hawkins that being acquired was strategically the best
option for making the Touchdown a success in the marketplace, and
moving the company towards achieving their vision. They agreed to a price
of $44 million, which compared to the $30 million valuation that Ericsson
had placed on the company was their best valuation to date. Dubinsky said:

> He absolutely committed to us that we would be independent. We would run
> the show. ...
>
> That was my personal turning point, when he said, "We're going to put what it
> takes behind this, even if it takes $15 million in marketing." To me, someone

who'd been looking for a million, a million, a million – ... that was huge. ... I was excited we had a future for Touchdown.[5]

Hawkins and Dubinsky also felt that being acquired would enable them to get back to their main jobs of developing the product and running the company, without constantly having to worry about the survival of the company and whether it would last long enough to launch their baby. Hawkins commented: "We wouldn't be sitting around, not knowing if we can launch the product. We could work on getting the product out."[6] Dubinsky also felt that the acquisition finally provided a long-term solution to their funding concerns, which would only have been temporarily mitigated by an investment by Compaq or Ericsson:

> We would have to turn right around and get more money after that because we would need to scale the company. I had been raising money full-time for three straight years, almost from the day I had joined Palm in '92. The thought of not having to raise money, and to focus on the business, was very appealing.[7]

While finding and negotiating the deal to be acquired comprised the Terminator role as it related to the ending of the company as an independent entity, perhaps the more difficult task was in relating these fundamental changes in the organization to the employees.

Despite the fact that Palm had less than 30 employees, and all of them had an ownership stake through stock options, the negotiations with U.S. Robotics were done in secret, with only Hawkins, Dubinsky, and one other Palm executive involved. In a situation such as this, the leader in the Terminator role must give great consideration to when, and how much, to tell employees of what is going on. Particularly for public companies, there are considerations such as the leakage of takeover rumors which could impact the stock price movements and subsequently affect the price and likelihood of a deal. However, for both public and private companies, there are internal considerations regarding the probable impact that the choice of how much and when to tell has on employees' behavior, both in terms of their motivation and work, and their likelihood of leaving the organization. Going through an acquisition can be a roller-coaster emotional experience for all those involved, and thus potentially very distracting and disconcerting for employees in an organization about to be acquired, or shopping itself around with acquisition in mind.

Unlike the situation of a temporary organization when everyone knows the ending before it happens, in an acquisition Terminators have to make the determination within their own context as to how open they are to employees with information about the prospects for the organization. On the one hand, being very open can enhance trust in the leadership of the organization, but at the same time increase the employees' exposure to the emotional roller-coaster as events unfold. On the other hand, remaining secretive about what is going on may either shield employees from the distraction of the emotional ups and downs, enabling them to continue with their day-to-day activities relatively freely, or it may increase speculation and rumor, making the situation worse. While generally most experts would be proponents of telling as much as you know when you know it, in fact this occurs relatively rarely. A Conference Board study on post-merger integration found that employees generally have very little information before a merger occurs, providing input in only a quarter of cases.[8] Which approach to take depends on any number of factors that are specific to each situation, but may also largely depend on the relationship between the leaders and the employees and the level of trust that exists between them. If a high level of trust exists between the employees and leadership, it is more feasible to keep the negotiations secret, with employees trusting the leaders' judgment in protecting the best interests of the company and the employees. At Palm, such a high level of trust existed, yet Dubinsky and Hawkins were still nervous about the employees' reaction to the news that they had been acquired.

Part of their concern lay in the general culture of Silicon Valley where they were located, where, even before the dot-com bubble of the late 1990s and into 2000, there was a certain cachet to working for a technology start-up, with the hope of a large payoff through a future initial public stock offering (IPO). This was what Silicon Valley tech employees dreamed of, not being in a small division of a giant corporation, and so the acquisition by U.S. Robotics might be seen as selling out to a corporate giant, where their work may be regarded as insignificant. Indeed, this was the reaction of a couple of the employees after they were told about the acquisition at a company-wide meeting. One told Dubinsky, "I wanted to work at a start-up, a small company – I've worked for big companies already. This is not what I came here for,"[9] while another said, "My attitude was, 'Let's make it on our own or die trying.'"[10] Indeed, Hawkins had called Art Lamb, who was Palm's first employee and was a key member of the Touchdown team, the night before as he was afraid that Lamb, an unpredictable personality, might react against the news and influence the other employees if he didn't have time to think about it first.

At the meeting, Dubinsky and Hawkins told the employees of the desperately needed funding and what the options had been, and why they felt the U.S. Robotics option was strategically the best option for Palm if it was to have a realistic chance of achieving its mission. The employees' reactions paralleled the concerns of Hawkins and Dubinsky in terms of their independence and the future of the product they were all deeply engaged in. Dubinsky and Hawkins gave reassurances that Palm would retain their independence. Dubinsky closed the meeting by stating:

> It's not clear that this is the best thing for us personally. What is clear is that this is the best thing for the product. This product deserves the best chance, and anything short of this would not give it the best chance. That's why we are doing this – even though I, personally, really don't want to sell the company.[11]

As it turned out, Dubinsky and Hawkins had correctly judged the attitude and reaction of the employees, with a result that none of them left Palm as a result of the acquisition by U.S. Robotics, and for the employees, with the exception of a U.S. Robotics logo appearing on their paychecks, life and work carried on as it had before. Now with the backing and resources of U.S. Robotics, Palm was able to focus on launching the Touchdown, which by its launch was renamed the Palm Pilot, and was hugely successful, dominating the market for PDAs. Clearly, the acquisition by U.S. Robotics had been the right strategic choice for Palm, enabling the launch of the product and the subsequent domination of the category before competitors were able to enter with effective competing products, a feat that Palm would have been very unlikely to achieve without the resources of the larger firm. Later, however, U.S. Robotics was itself acquired by 3Com Corporation, and Dubinsky and Hawkins, who became increasingly frustrated running Palm under a corporate umbrella, and failed to persuade 3Com to spin off Palm, left to return to the Creator role and form a new company, Handspring, which sold PDAs using the Palm operating system which it licensed from 3Com.

Variations in the Terminator Role

As we have now seen, the Terminator role, while always dealing with the ending of an organization in its original form, has some variations depending on whether or not the organization ceases to exist totally, or is absorbed into a larger organization. In the case of temporary organizations, there is a certainty of ending which is accompanied by a sense of a mission completed as the goals of the organization are fulfilled, thus there is no sense of shock or anxiety due to uncertainty which exists when an organization is acquired. Therefore the challenge for the Terminator of a temporary organization is in ensuring the sense of achievement and legacy for the organization and employees, and maintaining motivation and commitment as the organization winds down following the accomplishment of the organization's mission.

On the other hand, Terminators in organizations that are acquired have to manage the potentially damaging uncertainty that exists and lead the employees through the fear of the unknown. In doing so, Terminators face a difficult decision as to how much and when they tell employees of the impending acquisition. Anxiety caused by the unknown is perhaps the biggest hindrance to productivity, when organizations look for an organization to acquire them either as a strategic option or as a necessity for survival. Deciding whether information will ease or exacerbate this anxiety is a critical call for Terminators, and is made all the more difficult by the need to balance this consideration with other factors such as the possibility of rumors spreading outside the organization and destroying the acquisition opportunity completely. Thus the Terminator role varies with the specific emotions that need to be addressed in the organization, but are consistent in requiring skillful people-handling, motivation, and communication as well as the ability to bring closure to the independent organization.

Notes

1. Barry, Tom. 1997. Gold Medal Visionary. *Georgia Trend*, January 1, **12**(5).
2. Palm Computing example based on material in: Butter, Andrea, and Pogue, David. 2002. *Piloting Palm: The Inside Story of Palm, Handspring, and the Birth of the Billion-dollar Handheld Industry*. New York: John Wiley & Sons.
3. Butter, Andrea, and Pogue, David. 2002. *Piloting Palm: The Inside Story of Palm, Handspring, and the Birth of the Billion-dollar Handheld Industry*. New York: John Wiley & Sons, p. 113.
4. Ibid, p. 114.
5. Ibid, p. 109–11.
6. Ibid, p. 111.
7. Ibid, p. 106.
8. Schein, Lawrence, 2000. Post-Merger Integration: A Human Resources Perspective. Conference Board Research Report 1278-00-RR.
9. See note 3, p. 117.
10. Ibid.
11. Ibid, p. 116.

CHAPTER 7

Leadership Transitions

While it should now be apparent that the different phases of an organization's lifecycle require different leadership roles, it is important to look in more detail at how organizations transition from one phase to the next in the lifecycle, and in particular, the challenges that organizations can face in making these transitions. Indeed, these transition points often mark a danger zone in the life of an organization, and many organizations find their lifecycle terminally truncated by failing to successfully make the transition from one phase to the next. Figure 7.1 shows the three main danger points for an organization as it makes transitions through phases in the lifecycle. At each of these three points, there are specific dangers that organizations and leaders must overcome in order to avoid potentially lethal failure for the organization.

Transition from Creation to Growth Phase

Unfortunately, it is a common occurrence for an organization to fail to make the transition from the Creation to the Growth phase. Almost invariably, the cause of this early demise lies in the personality of the Creator, and particularly his or her inability to let go of their creation even if holding on results in the death of the organization. The strong sense of vision, to heroic proportions, that is held by the Creator, so vital to the initial success of the organization, can be a double-edged sword, making it difficult for the Creator to let go and move on, giving up the reins for somebody else to move the organization forward in the Accelerator role. The problem is that the leadership role required of the Creator is almost the antithesis of the role required of the Accelerator as the organization transitions from one where flexibility in responding to chaotic change is

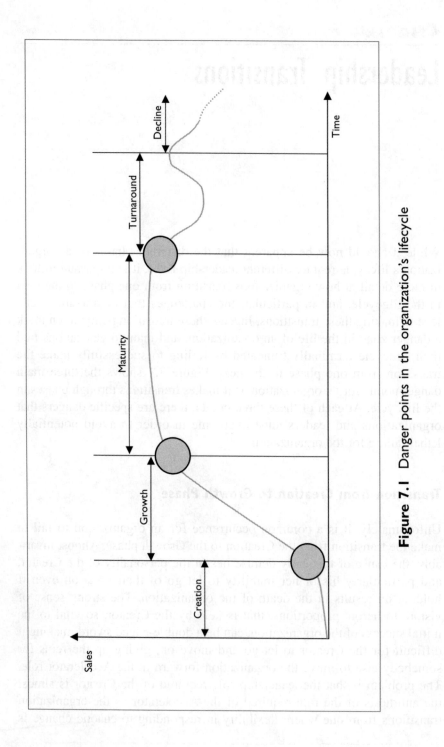

Figure 7.1 Danger points in the organization's lifecycle

replaced by a greater need for structure to allow growth to occur in an ordered manner without the organization spiraling out of control. Typically this takes a very different temperament in the Accelerator from that of the Creator, and thus frequently requires a change in leader in order for the organization to successfully make this transition. This can lead either to the Creator being forced to leave the organization, and bearing the pain of that separation, or, in staying, potentially causing the premature decline of the organization, and thus bearing the pain of an ultimately unfulfilled vision. Harvard's Rosabeth Moss Kanter and consultant Barry Stein observed in their book, *Life in Organizations*, that "there are many examples of entrepreneurs who seek their own immortality through organizations only to find their own presence seen by others as an obstacle to the organization's survival."[1]

Jeffrey Sonnenfeld, in his book *The Hero's Farewell*, examined how leaders exited organizations. One of his four types of exit was categorized as the Monarch, a leader who had to be forced out of the organization, or who held on to office until their death. These leaders, many of whom are entrepreneurial Creators, are so psychologically bound to their organizations that in their minds their identity is synonymous with that of the organization they have created, such that they cannot leave voluntarily or pass the organization on to someone who can more successfully take it to the next phase in its lifecycle. One such leader who Sonnenfeld interviewed was Bruce Henderson, founder of Boston Consulting Group (BCG), who captured this burden of the Creator:

> I think a lot of my problem with BCG is I care more about the company than I do about myself. I'll tell you, there is nothing more deadly than to have something that you put everything you have into – your marriage, your children, and all the other things – then you get told, "Get lost." Whatever you think is not only worthless, it's annoying. You can break somebody pretty easily that way.[2]

We see here that when the organization becomes a reality and the realization of the Creator's vision is within sight, the tremendous sense of mission held by the Creator can translate into a complete identification of the Creator with the organization. This brings us back to the Creator's need for immortality which drives the Creator in the first instance. Now that immortality becomes a possibility in the Creator's mind through the organization, a separation of the Creator from the organization is akin to death. In a famous, although tragic example, George Eastman, founder of Kodak, committed suicide when he realized that his contributions to his organization were at an end, leaving a suicide note that read: "My work is done, why wait?"

However, even with the strong identification of the Creator with the organization, in some instances the Creator can reconcile his or her separation from the organization, maintaining their identity with the organization even when separated from it, realizing that their imprint can remain with their organization. Steve Jobs, who himself was forcibly separated from Apple Computer, put it this way:

> To me, Apple exists in the spirit of the people that work there, and the sort of philosophies and purpose by which they go about their business. So if Apple just becomes a place where computers are a commodity item and where the romance is gone, and where people forget that computers are the most incredible invention that man has ever invented, then I'll feel I have lost Apple. But if I'm a million miles away and all those people still feel those things and they're still working to create the next great personal computer, then I'll feel that my genes are still here.[3]

It is essential for the Creator to be able to reach this type of perspective in order for the organization to successfully transition from the Creation to Growth phases of the lifecycle. If, however, the Creator fails to make this transition, then the issue may come down to one of power. If the Creator has retained effective domination of the company and there is no counterbalancing power to force the Creator to move on, then this poses a great danger to the organization's survival. On the other hand, if there is a countervailing power, such as a board of directors or venture capital interests, they may be forced into the difficult decision to remove the Creator in order to ensure the survival and progress of the organization.

Transition from Growth to Maturity Phase

The elixir of growth can become akin to an addictive drug to companies and the Accelerators that run them. In the constant quest to grow the organization, Accelerators risk the danger of continuing to push the "pedal to the metal" too long and too far, growing beyond the capacity of the market for their products or growing the organization beyond their capability to manage. When growth naturally slows down in the organization's core business, there is a great temptation for the Accelerator to maintain the organization's growth rate through other means, most often through acquisition. Often, these acquisitions start small, and may even be initially successful, at least from a financial perspective, especially for publicly traded high-growth companies where their stock is a liquid and highly valued currency.

Hanger Orthopedic Care, the largest provider of artificial limbs and braces in the U.S., and ranked number 74 on *Fortune* magazine's ranking of fastest growing companies in 1999, achieved a high rate of growth through a combination of organic growth and making small acquisitions. In the three years prior to making *Fortune*'s high-growth list, Hanger enjoyed an annualized growth rate of 63% in revenues and 51% in earnings per share. In 1998 it acquired 17 small, mainly family-owned businesses for a total of just over $25 million. Having reached the prestigious *Fortune* list and wishing to maintain a high growth rate, CEO Ivan Sabel made a giant leap by acquiring Hanger's largest competitor NovaCare for $445 million, a quantum leap from its prior acquisition experience. Predictably, the NovaCare acquisition proved much more difficult to integrate into the existing business than the smaller family businesses they had previously acquired. Sabel himself admitted: "We had never done something as large as NovaCare. We may have been more optimistic than we should have been."[4] As a result, Hanger plunged from profitability to loss, and their stock fell 74% in the year following the acquisition. The pressure brought to bear not only by the Accelerator's own expectations and hopes for growth, but also that of others in and outside the company can easily lead the Accelerator into the pursuit of growth that is ultimately perilous for the health and even survival of the company. Sabel had fallen into this trap of maintaining and even increasing growth expectations beyond what was feasible for the company, but maintained that the pressure from these increased expectations was to blame: "Investors want instant gratification, and we were not able to deliver."[5] Like the drug-addict, the growth-addict pursues instant gratification even though the short-term high can lead to disastrous long-term consequences.

Managing growth expectations is thus critical to the Accelerator, and is particularly critical when the organization is reaching the crest of the lifecycle, where growth is naturally slowing and the organization is preparing to move into the Maturity phase of the lifecycle. Just as an adolescent's growth rate slows as he or she approaches adulthood, so naturally will an organization's growth rate slow as it enters a corresponding phase in its lifecycle. Tempering the expectations for performance, however, can be a difficult task for many Accelerators, who often have difficulty seeing that the end of the company's Growth phase is at hand. Another company in the *Fortune* fast-growth company list in 1999 was Compuware which, ranked at number 29, had achieved an annualized growth rate of 40% in revenues and 100% in earnings per share over the previous three years. However, much of this growth had been due to the collective fear of the impending Y2K bug, prompting companies to spend millions of dollars preparing for a possible computer catastrophe. This helped the surge of sales at Compuware, which specializes in custom applications for mainframe computers and had an army of Y2K experts toiling away at client companies. Despite this foreseeable and definite ending to its growth prospects as the calendar turned from 1999 to 2000, in the fall of 1999, Compuware and CEO Peter Karmanos Jr. were still caught in the growth expectations' trap, telling analysts to expect continued growth of 35–40% for the year as it retrained its Y2K experts to become e-commerce consultants. Needless to say, with the smooth transition from 1999 to 2000 and the unfounded Y2K fears, and the subsequent bursting of the e-commerce bubble in April 2000, Compuware's growth went into a sudden reversal and the stock dropped 83% from $37.25 on December 31, 1999 to $6.25 at the close of 2000. While the slowdown in Compuware's growth rate was inevitable with the passing of the millennium, it was also predictable, and expectations could have been managed accordingly, and yet, seemingly Peter Karmanos Jr. and his team stuck to inflated expectations of their rate of growth. As Damian Rinaldi, an analyst who follows Compuware, told *Fortune:* "They stuck to a set of expectations that were much higher than they ultimately achieved for a couple of quarters too long. Karmanos got caught in the trap of continually raising the bar."[6]

Thus, as the organization's growth rate begins naturally to slow as the organization moves from the Growth to Maturity phase in the lifecycle, and as the leadership role consequently transitions from Accelerator to Sustainer, it is critical to manage expectations, both internally and externally, and allow the organization to make this natural transition without forcing growth beyond that which the market will allow.

Transition from Maturity to Decline Phase

Organizations decline and ultimately fail for a number of reasons. Many of these are financially driven, such as a lack of capitalization, poor management of cash flow or mistakes in investment. However, these types of financial error are typically more quickly fatal in small or fast-growing companies and pose dangers to companies in the Creation or Growth phases in the lifecycle, when an organization's prospects can be swiftly truncated by these mistakes and it has little cushion to fall back on. For companies that have progressed through the lifecycle and have enjoyed a substantial period of stability, financial distress is more likely to be a symptom than a cause of decline. Prompting the financial distress is a fundamental failure to adapt to changes in the organization's environment.

While change is a given in competitive environments, there are different types of change which can affect an organization's ability to adapt. Drastic, discontinuous change occurs when a fundamentally different technology substitutes for a product and wipes out the market for the old product. In such cases, mastery of the old technology does not confer competence in the new technology, and the firm's core competence is destroyed. Investment and mastery of the old technology may preclude the adaptation to the new technology and, from a market standpoint, it is efficient for the firms that dominated the old order to fall into rapid decline and out of existence. There are many examples of such technological discontinuities that prompt organizational failures, and indeed decimate entire industries, from the invention of refrigerators which destroyed thousands of ice companies, to the automobile, which replaced horse-drawn buggies, to the quartz watch, which decimated the Swiss watch industry, to the silicon semiconductor which rendered vacuum tubes obsolete. In each of these cases, the core competence in the substitute technology was very different from the core competence in the old technology, so that the expertise did not transfer to the new technology. In fact, sunk investment in the old technology would hinder a move to the new technology such that new players who developed or adopted the new technology could come in and dominate the market. These discontinuities, although significant, are rare, and usually transform entire industries, in a manner that the economist Joseph Schumpeter termed "creative destruction."[7] There is often little opportunity in such situations for a Transformer to revive the fortunes of the organization as their core competence is completely destroyed, although some firms may survive in a much reduced and specialist form, as, for example, some Swiss watch manufacturers did by gravitating exclusively to the luxury end of the market.

Interestingly, some discontinuous changes can be competence enhancing for some firms and competence destroying for others. For example, the advent and growth of digital cameras had a different impact on different companies. For camera manufacturers, we see that some have been able to adapt and become leaders in digital photography, such as Nikon and Olympus. Others, such as Pentax, are still exclusively devoted to film-based cameras. The difference is that the core competence of Olympus and Nikon was in lenses, and so they were not tied to film-based cameras and could still use their core competency in the new environment, whereas those companies which were more focused on the camera body and imaging onto film suffered. Perhaps the biggest casualty has been

Kodak, whose expertise in film has not helped them in moving to digital photography, despite an early recognition of the market's move to the new media and massive investment to try and move the organization in that direction. The expertise in the old media and the inertia that such competence creates within a large organization have resulted in massive losses and driven the company into decline. For other companies in industries related to digital technology, such as Sony in electronics or Ricoh in photocopiers, the rise in digital photography has been competence enhancing, enabling a new market opportunity to adapt and employ their technologies. Thus discontinuous change in substitute technologies can have very different impacts in moving firms along their lifecycles.

More common, however, than disruptive, discontinuous change are smaller changes in the environment. These small changes can actually be competence enhancing if they mesh with and improve the current technologies utilized by the organization. However, as companies become successful, and particularly as they sustain success for a prolonged period, there is a tendency for a degree of hubris to creep into the organization as the organization becomes convinced of its own infallibility. This tendency for a company's very success to sow the seeds of its decline was explored and explained by Danny Miller in his book *The Icarus Paradox: How Exceptional Companies Bring About Their Own Downfall*,[8] in which he paralleled once successful companies with the fabled Icarus of Greek mythology who, once successfully airborne, overconfidently flew too close to the sun, his wax wings melted, and he plunged into the sea. The power of Icarus's wings gave rise to the recklessness that doomed him. The paradox is that his greatest strength led to his demise. Similarly, the overconfidence of companies which enjoy stellar success often sows the seeds of their own failure by, among other things, excluding cues from the environment and ignoring developments not created internally, dismissing them as irrelevant, often called the "not invented here" syndrome. Miller writes:[9]

> It is ironic that many of the most dramatically successful organizations are so prone to failure. The histories of outstanding companies demonstrate this time and time again. In fact it appears that when taken to excess the very factors that drive success – focused tried-and-true strategies, confident leadership, galvanized corporate cultures, and especially the interplay among all these things – can also cause decline. Robust, superior organizations evolve into flawed purebreds; they move from rich character to exaggerated caricature as all subtlety, all nuance, is gradually lost.

Miller describes how successful companies take the traits that have made them successful, whether it be superior engineering, pioneering technology, brand building, or entrepreneurial organization building and pursue these strategies to extremes and to the exclusion of other factors that are essential to retain balance. Organizations become dominated by the function that has driven their success, and hubris develops, causing them to fail to see how their organization is losing touch with a changing environment, even leading them to believe that they shape the environment and do not need to be concerned with external changes. Thus, the heroic vision on which the organization was founded becomes a heroic self-concept whereby the organization becomes blind to its own faults and refuses to adapt to a changing environment.

The paradoxical part of this puzzle about the notion of heroic self-concept turning into declining performance, and why it is so easy to slip into this path, is that it is precisely by doing the things that made them successful initially which are the very things that can cause the downfall. It is a very fine line between the arduous pursuit of a characteristic such as quality, and an obsession with this characteristic that becomes destructive. The result is that it is very difficult for people inside the organization to spot when they are moving on this dangerous trajectory, because it appears that they are merely getting good at doing the right things. As a result, successful Transformers almost always have to come from outside the organization, in order to have a clear, unbiased view of the changes that need to be wrought on the organization and be free from internal political allegiances which may hinder changes in the status quo. A failure to spot this decline and appoint a Transformer to revitalize the organization will deny the organization the chance for a turnaround and can result in terminal decline.

Notes

1. Kanter, Rosabeth Moss, and Stein, Barry. 1979. *Life in Organizations: Workplaces as People Experience Them*. New York: Basic Books, p. 8.
2. Sonnenfeld, Jeffrey A. 1988. *The Hero's Farewell: What Happens when CEOs Retire*. New York: Oxford University Press, p. 84.
3. Lubenow, Gerald.C., and Rogers, Michael. 1985. Jobs talks about his rise and fall. *Newsweek*, September 30.
4. Kahn, Jeremy. 2000. Growth elixirs may be risky. *Fortune*, September 4, pp.164–70, p. 168.
5. Ibid.
6. Ibid, p. 166.
7. Schumpeter, Joseph. 1950. *Capitalism, Socialism, and Democracy*. New York: Harper.
8. Miller, Danny.1990. *The Icarus Paradox: How Exceptional Companies Bring About Their Own Downfall*. New York: HarperBusiness.
9. Ibid, p. 3.

CHAPTER 8

Spanning Roles

While the transition from one phase in the lifecycle to another often results in a change of leadership because the leadership roles at each phase are very different from one another, it is important to emphasize that the leadership roles of Creator, Accelerator, Sustainer, Transformer, and Terminator are roles and not individuals. As such it is entirely possible for a person to span multiple roles in an organization or over the course of the individual's career across multiple organizations. To illustrate this concept, we will take a more in-depth look at three individuals who have spanned multiple roles in their organizations.

Creator to Accelerator: Bill Gates at Microsoft

Bill Gates' first access to a computer came at age 13 when his high school, Lakeside High in Seattle, raised money to buy computer time on a mini-computer owned by a local General Electric facility. Gates and Paul Allen, a 15-year-old fellow student, became fascinated by the computer and what they could do with it. Soon the two of them were spending most of their free time on the computer and developing applications for it, such as a class-scheduling program for their school. Gates and Allen's first comm-ercial venture was a company they called Traf-O-Data which sold traffic flow reports to cities who were collecting data via rubber strips placed across key streets to monitor traffic flow, but had no simple way of analyzing the data collected. In their first year, they earned $20,000 from clients who included the state of Maryland and the Canadian province of British Columbia. However, after that first year, a similar service was intro-duced by the federal government with no charge to cities and Traf-O-Data's market evaporated.

However, Gates and Allen's fascination with computers continued, and they were sure that a computer revolution was about to happen. In the fall of 1973 Gates entered Harvard University, while Allen, who had gone to work for Honeywell in Seattle, arranged a transfer so that he could also be in Boston. Meanwhile, at Harvard, Gates also became friends with Steve Ballmer, who would later join Gates and Allen at the fledgling Microsoft.

Then, in December 1974, Allen's eye was caught by the January 1975 issue of *Popular Electronics* which had just hit the stands featuring the MITS Altair computer with the headline, "World's first minicomputer kit to rival commercial models." At a price of $397 to purchase the kit, based on the new Intel 8080 processor, the Altair generated a lot of excitement among computer hobbyists, not least of whom was Paul Allen. Allen rushed to find Gates and exclaimed "Look, it's going to happen! I told you this was going to happen! And we're going to miss it!"[1] While the Altair itself was a very basic machine with little capability, it was more what it represented which made it a milestone. As Gates later put it: "What excited us more than the kit itself was the realization that the personal computer miracle was going to happen."[2]

A week later, Gates and Allen called Ed Roberts, inventor of the Altair, and offered a version of the programming language BASIC for the Altair, which would make it much more accessible and useful to more people. Roberts was intrigued, and a few weeks later Allen flew to Albuquerque, New Mexico to demonstrate their software, even though neither Gates nor Allen had seen an actual Altair, but had developed the code based on an Altair-simulator Allen wrote for a larger computer, the DEC PDP-10 on which Gates had written the BASIC program. However, despite this obstacle, the program worked and the two licensed the program to Roberts, forming a company they initially called Micro-Soft, short for micro-computer software, to own the rights. Although they were very young, their youthful enthusiasm and capacity to work on their creation to the exclusion of virtually everything else overcame their lack of experience. Indeed, the industry itself was so early in its fledgling stage that even with their youth, Gates and Allen had as much experience as anyone else at the time, and the fluidity of the industry allowed them to dream big dreams with few constraints. In fact, Gates and Allen were insightful enough to figure out that the landscape of the personal computer industry might look very different from the computer industry as it then was. Gates recalled:

Back in 1975, everyone thought the personal computer industry would look very much like the entire computer industry did at the time – you'd buy your software from the company that built your computer. Few people even thought there would be a distinct "software industry." Paul and I disagreed. We believed that computing power would be cheap, that there would be computers everywhere made by lots of different companies, and that software would be needed to take advantage of these trends. So we decided to write and supply software for personal computers without getting involved in making or selling the hardware itself.[3]

With the contract agreed, Allen moved to Albuquerque to work for MITS and Gates joined him in the summer between his sophomore (second) and junior year. Although he went back to Harvard for his junior year, he kept returning to Albuquerque to work on improving his software, and eventually left Harvard, taking a leave of absence to rejoin Allen in Albuquerque and tried to interest other companies who were entering the fledgling microcomputer business in their software.

Microsoft began hiring its first employees in April 1976, hiring four programmers by the end of the summer, moving into a four-room office in Albuquerque, and focusing on writing software for the Intel chip that was in the Altair and other computers, as well as the first clone and competitor chips that were beginning to appear. At the time, Gates and his programmers were using terminals in their offices connected to a computer at the Albuquerque public school system and did their programming at all hours, especially at night when there were less users logged on to the system and so it responded faster. Although often unkempt and lacking formality or structure to their days, as is typical in young start-ups in the Creation phase, there was a high level of focus on what they were doing and where they were going. Gates captured the ambience of those early days:

> It was our life – we'd wake up, write code, maybe catch a movie, grab some pizza, write more code, and then fall asleep in our chairs.

> We were hard-core about writing code and selling software, and we didn't have much time to do anything else. This worked just fine for us, because our customers were hard-core computer enthusiasts who weren't bothered by a small feature set, a limited manual, or an advanced user interface. That was the way PC software was back then. Some companies shipped their software in plastic bags, with a one-page photocopied manual and a phone number that you could dial for "technical support." At Microsoft, when a customer called us to order some software, whoever answered the phone was the "shipping department." They'd run to the back of the office, copy a disk, put it in the mail, and then go back to their desk and write more code.[4]

By the end of 1978, Microsoft had 13 employees, over a million dollars in sales, and was growing at triple-digit rates. Microsoft was still in Albuquerque, but its attachment to MITS was gone. Ed Roberts had sold MITS in May 1977, and the new owner immediately claimed the rights to Microsoft's BASIC, resulting in a six-month trial which Microsoft won in December 1977. Microsoft was now selling its products to numerous computer manufacturers and Allen and Gates were not particularly attracted to Albuquerque. Many in the industry encouraged them to move to Silicon Valley, but Allen in particular wanted to move back to Seattle near his family and persuaded Gates, and so in January 1979, the company relocated to Bellevue, Washington, just outside Seattle. In June 1980, Steve Ballmer, Gates' friend from Harvard, joined Microsoft as assistant to the president, having graduated from Harvard and gained some marketing experience at Proctor & Gamble.

Even though Microsoft was moving up into the Growth phase of the organization, the company was propelled forward by a deal signed on November 6, 1980 to supply IBM with not just languages such as BASIC, but also an operating system for its first foray into the personal computer market. Gates, realizing that Microsoft did not have the time to develop a new operating system from scratch to match IBM's timetable, acquired the rights to an operating system called QDOS (Quick and Dirty Operating System), created by Tim Patterson who had previously worked with Microsoft in adapting their BASIC language for a card with Intel's new 8086 chip. Microsoft paid Patterson's employer, Seattle Computer Products, $50,000 for Patterson's QDOS, refined it, renamed it MS-DOS (Microsoft Disk Operating System), and licensed it to IBM. Importantly, Microsoft retained the rights to license MS-DOS to other computer manufacturers, correctly suspecting that the introduction of the IBM PC would legitimize the PC market and that other entrants would follow and the market would explode. Gates explained the deal and their strategy:

> We gave IBM a fabulous deal – a one time fee of about $80,000 that granted them the royalty-free right to use our operating system forever. Our goal was not to make money directly from IBM, but to profit from licensing MS-DOS to computer companies that wanted to offer machines compatible with the IBM PC. IBM could use our software, but it didn't have an exclusive license or control of future enhancements. This put Microsoft in the business of licensing operating system software to the personal computer industry.[5]

Just as Gates and Allen foresaw, the IBM PC was just the tip of the iceberg as, starting with Compaq, a string of clone makers appeared, all of whom licensed MS-DOS from Microsoft on a per machine basis. As a result, the market for PCs grew exponentially and with it Microsoft, such that at the time of the deal in 1980, IBM was 3,000 times the size of Microsoft, but by 1985 Microsoft had a larger market capitalization than IBM.

As Gates led Microsoft through this exponential growth curve, he had two overarching and related concerns: ensuring that Microsoft did not become insular but remained open to ideas from the market, and remaining vigilant at protecting Microsoft's dominant position in the industry by constantly being aware of new developments in the market-place. Indeed, many observers have described Gates as being almost para-noid about maintaining Microsoft's focus and dominance, to the extent of making dramatic "bet the company" changes in strategy when he sees the industry shifting, such as the move to a graphical interface with the intro-duction of Windows, and subsequently the .Net strategy as a response to the development and widespread use of the internet. Despite the success of Microsoft, Gates himself remains emphatic about the vulnerability of Microsoft's dominant position:

> [We need to retain] an underdog mentality that recognizes that every month there are dozens of companies who are started up with the sole goal of getting ahead of us or beating us in terms of sales of some of our products. Seeing that requires a certain amount of alertness that any slacking off, any decision that really isn't going to work out for the years ahead – eventually those will add up and you'll find yourself replaced in terms of all the key products. So you've got to want to reinvent the company and obsolete everything we've done as fast as possible.

> The advantages we have [due to our size and past success] are that we can bring in great people. And great people like to work with other great people, so you get a critical mass of really good research. Another nice thing is that customers love to tell us what they like about our products and how they'd like them changed – whether it's phone calls or in meetings we have with them, we can gather all of that data. Large organizations tend to move very slowly, and so the danger for us really isn't other large companies. I mean, I don't want to be complacent about them either, but they would not be anywhere near the top of my list. It's new companies that come along, that really have that clean page to focus on something new. And if we don't see it, figure out how to improve on it, take it in the right direction, then slowly but surely we'll fall behind.[6]

The effectiveness of Gates' and Microsoft's relentlessness in domin-ating much of the software industry not only provoked the ire of its competitors, but also the attention of regulators, prompting an investigation and subsequent anti-trust suit against Microsoft. At the same time, Microsoft's growth was naturally slowing due to saturation as PCs became ubiquitous, with growth rates declining to 16% in 2000 and 10% in 2001 from rates that averaged 38% throughout the 1990s. As Microsoft transitioned into the maturity phase, Gates was being pulled further and further from the product development side of the business, where he felt his leadership was most valuable. Thus, rather than playing the role of organizational Sustainer, in January 2000 he passed that role and the mantle of CEO on to Steve Ballmer, and became chief software architect, returning to the role of Creator at the product level, guiding development of the future products of the company.

Creator to Transformer: Steve Jobs at Apple Computer

Steve Jobs spent his childhood in Palo Alto, a town dominated at the time by one company, Hewlett-Packard, which had started in a garage a few years previously. Almost everyone worked for H-P, and spent their free time working in their own garages on their own pet electronics projects. Steve was not a particularly sociable person, but loved to spend time in his neighbors' garages, enthusing about the electronic wizardry he found there.

Although he was a quick learner and exceptionally bright, in school he was bored and unruly, spending his time on practical jokes and pranks. Through his friends and interest in electronics, he met up with Stephen Wozniak, a talented, mainly self-taught electronics buff, several years his senior. The two got along well and while Wozniak was at college at Berkeley and Jobs was still in high school, they produced a "blue box" device for tapping into AT&T's telephone network to make long distance calls for free. The two of them produced these "blue boxes", selling them to students at a large profit. It symbolized the anti-establishment, prankster attitude that they both shared and that would influence what was to come.

Later, Jobs went to Reed College, but dropped out after a year. He continued to stay on the campus and to study informally without being enrolled. He was also involved in drugs, eastern religions, and experimental diets, all products of the late 1960s and early 1970s movements going on in California.

Wozniak and Jobs were also both members of the Homebrew Computer Club, a hobbyist club for those interested in electronic design in the Palo Alto area, where people would come together and share their latest ideas and inventions. Wozniak was very interested in this and spent endless hours developing designs to show off at the meetings. Jobs, however, had a greater interest in the commercial aspect of these potential products. As Wozniak recalled:

> When I got going in the Homebrew Computer Club, I started telling Steve about these microprocessors. And he kept asking, "Can it do a disk operating system?" Yes, you could add a floppy disk. You can add a disk or something. "Can it do time-sharing system?" Well, theoretically, you can do anything because it's a computer, but it was hard to tell him what the limits of this starting little machine were. All I wanted in my heart was a machine that could run a programming language ... He was always thinking way out there, to machines that were closer to the ones he had seen in companies that actually had marketability and dollars associated with them. ... To me, I just liked designing computers. The better computer I design, the better step I've made. Steve's thinking business and business opportunities you've got to take advantage of, so he basically went out and started talking to interested parties.[7]

Thus Wozniak and Jobs teamed up and eventually produced a design for a machine that they called the Apple I. They founded a partnership with each of them having 45% and Wayne, another friend from the club, having the remaining 10%. Steve then went out to sell this machine, and came across an electronics store owner who wanted to expand into the fledgling computer market, and agreed to buy 50 machines at $500 each. Apple Computer was born. Subsequently, Steve went around negotiating supplies, and they used the Jobs family home to assemble the components to fill the order.

After this first delivery, Steve wanted to build another 50 on spec, convinced that he could sell them. Wayne, however, had no confidence in this idea and could only see himself becoming liable for the 10% of the debts that they were likely to accrue from the order of new parts. He renounced his stake in the venture and Wozniak and Jobs went ahead and built the machines. Over the first year they sold about 190 machines for approximately $95,000, about half of which was profit.

With this success behind them, Wozniak began working on an improved machine. Up to this point the Apple I and other machines that were appearing as computers for hobbyists required self-assembly and therefore a reasonable degree of expertise and interest to put together, Jobs' vision was for a machine that could reach a broader audience:

> The Apple I took us over a big hurdle, but a lot of people who wanted to use the product were unable to. We were getting some feedback from a fairly small

sample – maybe 40, 50 people. We were hearing from dealers, too. They'd say, "I think we can sell 10 times more of these if you would just put a case and keyboard around it." That's where a lot of the direction for the Apple II came from. ... We were thinking we should build a computer you could just roll out of the box and use. There were a lot more software hobbyists than hardware hobbyists around, and we could satisfy a lot more people if they didn't have to be hardware hackers to use it.[8]

In order to do this, Jobs needed a specially designed case with a keyboard, and for that he required capital. So Jobs went in search of venture capital and found it in the form of Mike Markkula, who had made his fortune by working at Intel when it went public in the early 1970s. Markkula saw the potential for the Apple II and invested $91,000 in cash, plus a personal guarantee for a further $250,000 line of credit in exchange for a 30% interest in the newly formed Apple Computer. The Apple II was formally introduced to the world on April 6, 1977, at the West Coast Computer Fair. It was an instant success.

The fledgling company grew rapidly and raised funds through some key venture capitalists in the area, who became board members, adding further management expertise. Although Wozniak had been the designer for Apple I and II, Jobs was clearly the playing the Creator role for the organization, drawing in attention and resources, having the vision for a machine which would be of wider interest than to just the fanatical hobbyists at the Homebrew Computer Club. While the Apple II was an astounding success, reaching into corporate America thanks to Visi-Calc – a software program designed for the Apple II and the first spreadsheet which revolutionized financial tasks in the office – Apple Computer, and particularly Jobs, were aware that, in this rapidly changing environment, the Apple II would only have a shelf life of a few years. Jobs also wanted to create a machine that was all his, as the credit for the Apple II went mainly to Wozniak. In December 1979, Jobs received an invitation to visit Xerox's research center, Xerox PARC, where they had an experimental computer, the Alto, which had a graphical user interface and a mouse. Jobs was immediately enthralled with this new possibility for where the computer might go:

When I went to Xerox PARC in 1979, I saw a very rudimentary graphical user interface. It wasn't complete. It wasn't quite right. But within 10 minutes, it was obvious that every computer in the world would work this way someday. And you could argue about the number of years it would take, and you could argue about who would be the winners and the losers, but I don't think you could argue that every computer in the world wouldn't eventually work this way.[9]

For Jobs, seeing the graphical user interface of the Alto took his vision of computers for a wider, non-technical audience to the next level. Here was the possibility of a computer that anyone could use without technical or computer language training. Jobs went back to Apple and got 100 engineers together to develop a machine called Lisa, named after his daughter, based on what he had seen at Xerox PARC. However, developing the graphical user interface proved more difficult than they imagined and problems and development costs were escalating. The required selling price of the Lisa rose to around $10,000, making it too expensive for most PC users. Also, the new people that Jobs had brought in to work on Lisa were mainly classically trained computer engineers from established companies such as H-P and Xerox, which caused a culture clash with the "hacker" generation of the early Apple. This caused numerous conflicts between the Lisa group and the rest of Apple, with the Lisa people taking a superior attitude, despite the fact that all of Apple's revenues were derived from the Apple II. Finally the board decided that enough was enough and reorganized the company, removing Jobs from the Lisa project. Yet Jobs' vision of a simple-to-use graphics-based computer that could reach a mass audience remained ingrained in him and, after brooding for a few months, Jobs stumbled across a project for a smaller, consumer-oriented computer called Macintosh being developed by one of their engineers, Jeff Raskin. The board, thinking that this obscure project would keep Jobs from interfering with Apple II and Lisa, put him in charge of the Macintosh despite the objections of Raskin. However, for Jobs, ever the Creator, this missionary zeal to achieve his vision was merely transposed onto the Macintosh project and he essentially formed a company within Apple, separating his group from the rest of the company, even hoisting a pirate flag over their building. For Jobs and his team, the Macintosh would bring computers into the everyday world of ordinary people, democratizing the power of computers which had been the reserve of a few:

A hundred years ago, if somebody had asked Alexander Graham Bell, "What are you going to be able to do with a telephone?" he wouldn't have been able to tell the ways that the telephone would affect the world. But remember that the first public telegraph was inaugurated in 1844. It was an amazing breakthrough in communications. You could actually send messages from New York to San Francisco in an afternoon. People talked about putting a telegraph on every desk in America to improve productivity.

But it wouldn't have worked. It required that people learn this whole sequence of strange incantations, Morse code, dots and dashes, to use it. It took about 40 hours to learn. The majority of people would never learn to use it. So fortunately, in the 1870s, Bell filed the patents for the telephone. It performed basically the same function as the telegraph, but people already knew how to use it. Also, the neatest thing about it was that besides allowing you to communicate with just words, it allowed you to sing, to intone your words with meaning beyond the simple linguistics.

And we're in the same situation today. Some people are saying that we ought to put an IBM PC on every desk in America to improve productivity. It won't work. The special incantations you have to learn this time are "slash qzs" and things like that. They are not going to learn "slash qzs" any more than they're going to learn Morse code. The current generation of computers just won't work any longer. We want to make a product like the first telephone. We want to make mass-market appliances. That is what the Macintosh is all about. It's the first telephone of our industry. And, besides that, the neatest thing about it to me is that the Macintosh lets you sing the way the telephone did. You don't simply communicate words, you have special print styles and the ability to draw and add pictures to express yourself.[10]

The Mac team was about 25 strong by early 1982. They were all opinionated, dedicated, and convinced they could build a better computer than anyone else. They cared more about shocking the world with their amazing computer than ordinary career objectives such as promotions or compensation, and were working at a pace to bring it to fruition within two years.

As a Creator, and with the vision he had that the Macintosh would be remembered in history the same way that the telephone was, Jobs had a clear quest for immortality which he imbued in his team. Each of the 30 or so members of the team as of July 1982 signed their names on the final shop drawing for the Mac. The handwritten names were made a permanent part of the mold, so that the signatures were on the inside of every Macintosh produced. In this symbolic action, Jobs captured the reasons they were all working on the machine; for the impact they believed they would have on the world.

In January 1984, after a last superhuman effort by the team, the Mac was launched and introduced to the public with one of the most acclaimed commercials of the decade, airing during the Superbowl. Apple sold more than 70,000 Macintosh computers in the first 100 days, more than any other computer before it.

However, the euphoria of the launch of Macintosh didn't last long. While the Macintosh was way ahead of the IBM PC and its clones in terms of ease of use and graphics, by this time a whole array of software had been developed for the PC and the Macintosh was lacking basic programs such as a spreadsheet and database. Thus by the fall of 1984, sales were already slipping below projections. John Sculley, who had been brought to Apple from Pepsi by Jobs to run the overall company as CEO, began to feel that Jobs was not the right person to continue to run Macintosh, but wanted him to return to a Creator role for future new products as head of Apple Labs. Jobs, who was still chairman of the board, felt that he was being pushed out of an operating role and a bitter dispute arose between Jobs and Sculley. The board also took the view that Jobs was essentially a Creator and saw Sculley, with his background in marketing at Pepsi, more able to take on the Accelerator role that the company now needed if it was to continue on its growth path. At the end of May, 1985, Jobs was ousted from the company he founded.

After a summer of reflection, Jobs jumped back into a Creator role, recruiting half a dozen people he had worked with at Apple to form NeXT Computer, to create a powerful personal computer designed for the higher education market. After four years of development, the first NeXT computer rolled off the fully automated production line. It was a highly advanced machine, packaged in a sleek black cube, incorporating technologies that no other personal computer had at the time, such as a recordable CD drive and an advanced display that allowed for greater resolution and used the same software technology as laser printers, so what you saw on the screen was exactly what printed on the page. However, while aimed solely at the education market, it was priced beyond the means of students and found limited acceptance from researchers and faculty. In over four years, NeXT sold just 50,000 computers, and discontinued making the machines in 1993. However, the company continued, focusing on software, and particularly the operating system, Nextstep, which had been developed for the NeXT computer. NeXT ambled along with revenues of about $50 million per year, posting an annual profit just once.

Meanwhile however, Apple had problems of its own. Having gone through a period of growth under Sculley, where annual revenues had grown from less than $2 billion when Jobs left in 1985, to almost $8 billion in 1993, Apple had subsequently had a truncated Maturity phase and plunged into a tailspin, eventually firing three CEOs in four years, starting with Sculley in 1993. By 1996, with Gil Amelio at the helm, sales were down 11% year-on-year and the company lost $816 million. Inside the company, the position was perhaps even bleaker, as the next generation operating system, code named Copland, which was needed to respond to Microsoft's introduction of Windows 95, had had to be scrapped due to overwhelming development problems. The company had even been shopping itself around, with the thought of being acquired by IBM or Sun, but neither of these deals came to fruition. The company also looked around to purchase an operating system and had been in negotiations to purchase Be Inc, a software company founded by former head of Apple's software development, Jean-Louis Gassée, but when those negotiations broke down, Amelio turned to NeXT and, in December 1996, purchased NeXT and the consulting services of Jobs for $400 million.

Over the next few months, however, the pressure on Amelio increased, with media reports highly critical of Apple's performance frequently appearing, such as a feature story in *Fortune* magazine titled, "Something's Rotten in Cupertino"[11] (Cupertino is where Apple's headquarters is located). Many of these stories were looking towards Steve Jobs as the person to turn Apple around, a view which was adopted by the board, who, to few people's surprise, ousted Amelio in July 1997, leaving Jobs in the Transformer role of the organization.

Jobs immediately focused on the three key constituencies of Apple: external software developers; employees; and customers. These three constituencies were vital as momentum had shifted away from Apple in the marketplace, as reflected by their declining share of the personal computer market. These constituencies were losing faith in Apple and their reasons for staying with Apple, and if they left, Jobs knew it could result in the death of Apple. Developers, facing a shrinking market for Apple's products, and hence their own, were switching their investments to developing exclusively for Windows, without bothering to put the extra effort into making Mac versions of their software. Employees were becoming increasingly demoralized after a series of restructurings, layoffs, cancelled projects, and a revolving door at the top of the organization. Customers perceived that Apple's ease of use advantage was diminishing with the introduction of Windows 95, and more and more corporate customers were standardizing around the Windows platform and cutting support for Macintosh. Even in Apple's core market, education, where the majority of students and teachers used Macintoshes, doubts were beginning to arise as concern rose that students should be trained on the same computers they were likely to encounter in the workplace. As Jobs, uncharacteristically lost for words, admitted to a *Time* magazine reporter: "Apple has some tremendous assets, but I believe without some attention, the company could, could, could – I'm searching for the right word – could, could, die."[12]

Four weeks after Amelio was fired, Jobs took the stage at the MacWorld Expo in Boston and delivered a rousing speech which addressed all three of his key constituents with the aim of restoring the Apple's credibility to them, and giving a positive reason to each as to why they should continue to trust in Apple. He began by praising the demoralized employees, emphasizing that Apple's woes were not their fault. He stated that indeed Apple had great people, but had been guided in the wrong direction:

> Apple is executing wonderfully on many of the wrong things. The ability of the organization to execute is really high, though. I've met some extraordinary people at Apple. There's a lot of great people at Apple. They're doing some of the wrong things because the plan has been wrong. … So what I see is the makings of a very healthy company with some extraordinarily talented people who are still just as passionate and committed to the dream of computing as they ever were. They need to come together and get a great plan and then start to execute it. That's exactly what's been happening over the last four weeks.[13]

Jobs went on to spend the bulk of his speech on how Apple needed to refocus back to its core competence and markets, and how some of the insularity or hubris which had developed at Apple needed to be recast, and that Apple had to look outside to work with partners rather than shunning them. He zeroed in on the two market segments that Apple still dominated, the creative professions, such as graphic design and publishing, and education:

> So, you're going to see Apple proactively focusing much more on these two markets where it is very relevant. And both of these markets are growing over 20 percent a year. Now Apple share is shrinking in these markets slowly, but I think you're going to see that stabilize and turn around. You're going to see Apple grow with these markets because it's going to do a much better job of focusing [on] where its relevance is and where its legacies lie.[14]

As an example of how Apple was shunning its best allies and not taking advantage of potential synergies with software developers, he spoke of how Apple was failing to work with Adobe, whose software was the de facto standard in the publishing and graphic design segment:

> Something like ten- to fifteen-percent of Mac sales can be traced directly back to people using Adobe Photoshop as their power application, right? When was

the last time you saw Adobe and Apple co-marketing Photoshop? When was the last time we went to Adobe and said, "How do we make a computer that will run Photoshop faster?" These things haven't been as cohesive as they should have been. I think we're going to start proactively focusing much more on how we do these things.[15]

In the same vein, the biggest announcement that Jobs made in the MacWorld Expo speech, and the most significant early move of his turn-around of Apple, was a deal with Microsoft whereby Microsoft invested $150 million in Apple, committed to continue producing Office for Mac and other software and entered a cross-licensing agreement which ended the disputes between the two companies, paying Apple a reported further $100 million. Despite the hisses and boos that this announcement received from some of the gathered Apple faithful, this agreement did much to restore Apple's credibility among both software developers and corporate and education customers who saw this as evidence that Apple had a viable future as a second platform. But in making this alliance, Jobs made it clear that Apple could no longer externalize the blame for its own failings, and that while external relationships were necessary in turning Apple around, responsibility for making the turnaround work lay clearly in their own hands:

> Right now we're shepherding some of the greatest assets in the computer industry. And if we want to move forward and see Apple healthy and pros-pering again, we have to let go of a few things here.
>
> We have to let go of this notion that for Apple to win, Microsoft has to lose. For Apple to win, Apple has to do a really good job. And if others are going to help us, that's great. Because we need all the help we can get. And if we screw up or we don't do a good job, it's not somebody else's fault. It's our fault. So I think that's a very important discussion. I think if we want Microsoft Office on the Mac, we'd better treat the company that puts it out with a little bit of gratitude. We like their software.
>
> So, the era of setting this up as a competition between Apple and Microsoft is over, as far as I'm concerned. This is about getting Apple healthy and this is about Apple being able to make incredibly great contributions to the industry to get healthy and prosper again.[16]

Finally, Jobs talked about the Apple brand, and the values and vision that defined the company, ushering in the "Think different" advertising campaign which would recapture the original vision of Apple in making computers that would change the world. For the campaign, Jobs rehired TBWA\Chiat\Day, the advertising agency who had come up with the Superbowl commercial which had launched the original Macintosh, but who had been fired as Apple's agency when Jobs was fired from Apple back in 1985. In closing his MacWorld speech, Jobs clearly articulated what Apple was originally about, and where it was once again headed:

> Lastly, I want to just talk a little bit about the Apple brand and what it means to a lot of us. You know, I think you always have to be a little different to buy an Apple computer. When we shipped the Apple II, you had to think different about computers. Computers were these things you saw in movies. They weren't these things you have on your desktop. You had to think differently because there wasn't any software at the beginning. You had to think differently when a first computer arrived at a school, where there had never been one before. It was an Apple II.

> I think you [had to really think] differently when you bought a Mac. It was a totally different computer working in a totally different way, using a totally different part of your brain. It opened up the computer world for a lot of people who thought differently. You were buying a computer with an installed base of one. You have to think different to do that.

> I think you still have to think differently to buy an Apple computer. And I think the people that do buy them do think differently. They are the creative spirits in this world. They are the people who are not just out to get a job, but they're out to change the world. They're out to change the world using whatever great tools they can get. We make tools for those kinds of people.

> So hopefully, what you've seen here today are some beginning steps that give you some confidence that we, too, are going to think differently and serve the people that have been buying our products since the beginning. Because a lot of times, people think they're crazy. But in that craziness, we see genius. And those are the people we're making tools for.[17]

The speech set the tone for the turnaround of Apple, helping to restore the confidence of developers, employees, and customers, but the rhetoric also needed to be backed up by concrete actions. Over the next year or so, some of those concrete actions became apparent. He purged the board who had overseen Apple's decline, leaving only two outsiders who were relatively new to the board, and adding new board members who had considerable computer industry experience. He sifted through the multitude of products that were being haphazardly developed, refining the development focus to only those potentially high-impact products that would address their core markets. Almost a year to the day after the MacWorld Expo speech, Apple launched its first iMac computer aimed at the consumer and education markets. It was a big hit, recapturing some of its lost market share, particularly in the consumer market. Apple effectively focused its product offerings into four segments; a desktop and laptop for the professional and consumer markets. Net income at Apple went from a loss of over $1 billion in the year ended September 30, 1997, to a profit of $309 million in 1998, $601 million in 1999 and an Apple record $786 million in 2000.

Transformer to Accelerator to Sustainer: Robert W. Woodruff at The Coca-Cola Company

When Robert Woodruff was appointed President of The Coca-Cola Company in 1923, the company was in serious trouble and potentially in danger of going bankrupt. The company had been founded in 1886 by John Styth Pemberton,[18] a chemist who concocted medicines and other pharmaceutical products, who saw the growth of soda fountains, often within drug stores, and saw an opportunity to use his skills to develop a drink to sell by the glass in fashionable soda fountains. Pemberton developed a syrup, named by his bookkeeper, Frank Robinson, as "Coca-Cola" and sold it to soda fountains to dilute and sell by the glass. As folklore has it, one day a busy soda vendor, to save himself a few steps to the fresh water tap, diluted the syrup with soda water and a new drink was born, which became exceedingly popular. Pemberton patented the syrup and Coca-Cola became the first trademarked beverage on the market. That first year, Pemberton sold 25 gallons of syrup, and with the popularity of soda fountains continuing to grow, growth prospects were good. However, Pemberton's health failed him, and in order for the sales of the drink to continue, from his sickbed he sold a two-thirds interest in Coca-Cola, plus the equipment to make it, to his friend George Lowndes and Willis Venable, a clerk at Jacob's Drug Store, for the grand sum of $1483.29. However, Lowndes and Venable had no further capital to invest in launching the product and so it lay dormant until their interests were bought out by other friends of Pemberton's, Woolfork Walker, Asa Candler, and Joe Jacobs, the owner of Jacob's Drug Store. Four months before Pemberton's death in 1888, this group bought out Pemberton's remaining interest for $550. Soon afterwards Candler bought out his partners, and for $2,300 became the sole owner of The Coca-Cola Company.

Candler set about growing the company through extensive advertising and sales and by 1895 Coca-Cola was a nationally available product. While Candler was growing the business through soda fountain sales, some of his customers were extending their business by making ready-made drinks of Coca-Cola and putting it in bottles for home consumption. Candler was unimpressed by the potential of this business, and he gave away the bottling rights for most of the country for the nominal sum of one dollar, resulting in the founding of The Coca-Cola Bottling Company. Sales soared, both on the fountain side and the bottled side, and bottling franchises sprung up all over the country. This in turn resulted in imitators springing up trying to ride on Coca-Cola's success. By 1916, there were no less than 153 imitators of Coca-Cola, with every conceivable corruption of the Coca-Cola name, such as Coke-Ola, Kok-Kola, Cofa-Cola, and even Coca & Cola. In order to distinguish Coca-Cola from its imitators, a distinctive bottle was developed, based on the shape of the cocoa bean. It was an instant success and has since become the best-known product package in the world.

In the same year Candler stepped down from running Coca-Cola in order to pursue his political ambitions, the following year being elected as mayor of Atlanta. He also divided his stock among his wife and five children, who immediately put the company up for sale. In September 1919, a syndicate, headed by Ernest Woodruff, Robert's father, purchased the company for $15 million in cash and $10 million in preferred stock. Almost immediately the company went public, issuing 500,000 shares at $40 a share.

However, the company was already headed towards dire financial trouble. One of the primary reasons was the price of sugar. The bottlers had a contract with the company for the price of their supply of syrup, a price calculated on the price of sugar at around 6¢ per pound. However, World War I caused the price of sugar to escalate to 28¢ per pound, leaving the company making a loss on supplying its only product, and the bottlers refused to allow the company to increase the price of the syrup, even going to court to ensure that the company continued to supply the bottlers at the contracted price. To make matters worse, fearing the price would rise even higher, the company placed forward contracts for millions of dollars for the future supply of sugar. However, when rationing ended at the end of the war, instead of rising, sugar dropped back to 18¢ per pound, leaving the company paying over market price for its sugar supply. Eventually, the company was able to negotiate a higher price with the bottlers, based on the compelling argument that if the company went bankrupt, there would be no more syrup and consequently no more business for anyone.

However, the damage was done, reflected in the fact that the stock had dropped by more than half to $18 a share.

One of the stockholders was Robert Woodruff, who had borrowed heavily to invest in the initial offering of the stock, purchasing more than 3,500 shares. Already a successful salesman with the White Motor Company, Woodruff was persuaded to take on the presidency of Coca-Cola at a salary of $36,000 per annum – $50,000 less than he was already making at his current employer. As he put it:

> The only reason I took that job was to get back the money I had invested in Coca-Cola stock. I figured that if I ever brought the price of stock back to what I had paid for it, I'd sell and get even. Then I'd go back to selling cars and trucks.[19]

On taking over the reins, Woodruff first set about stemming the tide of declining sales, which had dropped from 19 million gallons of syrup in 1919 to 15 million in 1922, by addressing what he considered the underlying cause, the inconsistent quality of the product. This was caused by an inconsistency in the water quality used, bottles which were improperly washed, and fountains and production facilities which were unclean. He instituted quality control procedures and a sales structure to the organization. In a memo to his board of directors,[20] almost a year to the day of taking over the reins, Woodruff outlined the steps he had taken as a Transformer to reverse the decline in sales and the foundations of his role as Accelerator in putting in place an infrastructure that would enable the company to continue to grow. The memo details the institution of a quality control process, noting that "Standardization of our product is vital to success, and with this view we have established as perfect laboratory and manufacturing control as is humanly possible." It also covered the progress that the legal department had made in terms of eliminating imitators. Due to the cost structure of the business, Woodruff also detailed how personnel were being reduced in some departments, how the purchase of sugar was now being secured at market or below market rates, and how the loss-making Canadian and Cuban businesses were being separated out and restructured.

On laying the foundation for future growth, Woodruff detailed to his board how a sales infrastructure was being developed and how partnerships were being made with the independent bottlers to increase the advertising at shared cost. Importantly, he also persuaded the bottlers not to carry any other nationally advertised drinks, thus laying the groundwork for an exclusive national distribution infrastructure which would be difficult to emulate. He concludes his memo by asking his directors to consider whether or not to grow the company through the development of other brands, through vertical integration and expansion abroad, concluding:

> all of these things must give us thought and concern, for in the light of experience and in view of tendencies and progress which may be made in the next few years, each and every one of these items will inevitably meet us face to face, and we should walk in their direction that we may meet them rather than waiting for them to meet us. I ask for your help and counsel in meeting them.

Unlike Candler, Woodruff saw the growth potential for Coca-Cola in bottles at least as much, if not more, than in the soda fountain. Although the fountain side of the business was by far the larger when he took over, he knew that his desire to "make Coca-Cola available to anyone, anywhere in the world, whenever they want one, and be certain that it tastes just like the last Coca-Cola they drank"[21] could only be achieved through developing the bottling side of the business. To this end, he spent a lot of time building relationships with the independent bottlers and finding ways that they could join together in promoting the product.

He also pushed forward with overseas expansion, despite the reluctance of his board to invest heavily in this area. Indeed, it is thought that the only time the board ever denied a request from Woodruff was during the first two years of his tenure when he wanted funds to expand overseas. Woodruff, however, ploughed ahead anyway with whatever funds he could appropriate, and set up an foreign department in New York, well away from the Atlanta headquarters, where special export bottles were sold to ships in New York harbor. Not long afterwards, calls began coming in from all over the world from foreign bottlers wishing to gain the rights to bottle Coca-Cola in their home markets. Within five years the New York branch was officially incorporated as The Coca-Cola Export Corporation and the drive to become available "at arm's reach" anywhere in the world was on. Bottling plants began to be set up around the world, with franchises always being given to respected businesspeople who would strive for the same quality of product that Woodruff insisted upon.

Despite the success and growth of Coca-Cola, Woodruff was never content with what had already been achieved, preferring to dwell not on the past successes, but on the future opportunities. Even as he was in the Accelerator role, and growth was occurring at a rapid pace, Woodruff was concerned with the possibility of complacency creeping into the organization. To celebrate the fiftieth anniversary of the founding of Coca-Cola, a dinner was held at the exclusive Piedmont Driving Club in Atlanta.

Against this celebratory mood in this elegant setting, Woodruff began his remarks:

> Any semi-centennial anniversary causes a feeling of pride at the existence through fifty years, of the product or the company or the relationship that is commemorated. I wish I could fully share that feeling concerning this occasion that we meet to mark tonight. I can't. My feeling is rather one of dissatisfaction – or perhaps unsatisfaction, if that is a word – about us, you and me, for not having done more than we have through these past years.

> To an individual, a half century means that most of his years are behind. He can begin to see over the crest of the hill and down the far side. But in the life of Coca-Cola, fifty years has no such significance at all. For at their close we are still at its beginning, we are still pioneers. ...

> All of us as we travel about, hear talk of the success of Coca-Cola and The Coca-Cola Company; and that is always embarrassing to me because it makes me conscious of our shortcomings – of how much more our opportunities might have enabled us to accomplish. Relatively, in comparison to some companies, ours might be said to be successful, but remember this: no other company has had Coca-Cola. ...

> I know that we all have the feeling that now is a good time to pat ourselves on the back a little bit – to admit to ourselves how good we are. And we wouldn't care if the rest of the world found that out. But in that feeling lies the greatest danger that has ever faced this organization.

> The history of American business shows that many had their little day of glory, a day of patting themselves on the back. But where are the great houses of yesterday? I think I know what their trouble was – what caused their downfall. They thought they had arrived and could afford to rest awhile and draw pensions. There are no old soldiers homes for business concerns. For them, the war goes on.

> They had only reached the point at which many are called and few are chosen. Failure of their managements to realize that they had only reached a point from which to start resulted in their rejection. ...

> We have arrived, but where? Only to a place from which to begin to do things. Our opportunities are greater, but that is all. More will be required of us. From this point on, the race grows swifter. ...

> If we get to thinking that the hard days are over and that now all we have to do is to hold what we have, then the days of real tribulation begin. Not realizing

what is happening to us, but knowing something is badly wrong, we will begin
to lose confidence in one another and to blame one another. ...

We worked 50 years for opportunity. Now we have it. What are we going to do
with it?[22]

The advent of World War II, and the U.S. entering the war following the
attack on Pearl Harbor in December 1941, prompted a decision that had a
far-reaching impact on the worldwide growth of Coca-Cola. In the months
immediately prior to the U.S. entering the war, Woodruff, recalling the sugar
situation during World War I which had almost resulted in the bankruptcy of
the company, began securing and stockpiling sugar. However, with the
advent of the war, and the subsequent rationing of sugar, Woodruff decided
that the company would share a portion of its stockpile with both people at
home and the men in uniform, regardless of where they were. Woodruff
pledged that the company would make Coca-Cola available to every
member of the armed services wherever they were at the same price as it had
always been at home – a nickel. Woodruff's offer was enthsiastically greeted
by the Department of Defense, and portable bottling plants were developed,
logistics for the supply of syrup established and Coca-Cola plants followed
the troops wherever they went, becoming an essential piece of military
equipment almost on a par with ammunition.

The result of this after the war was not only a great affection for the drink
among returning soldiers, but a legacy from the war of 64 bottling plants
spread throughout the world ready to supply the local populations.

The growth of the company during and following the war propelled
Coca-Cola to worldwide dominance in the soft drink industry. However,
even as the growth rate inevitably slowed and The Coca-Cola Company
grew into the maturity phase of the lifecycle, Woodruff always remained
alert and on guard against the possibility of a heroic self-concept creeping
into the organization. The main challenge, as Woodruff saw it, and indeed
the general challenge companies face in the maturity phase, was to
balance the essential wisdom and value embodied in the traditions of the
company, while not being bound by them and unwilling to take risks in
order to continue to grow the organization. As he brought in new
management to run the day-to-day operations of the company following
the war years, he warned:

Many people seem to have the idea that once a business becomes an established success, all you've got to do is sit tight and ride along with the tide and
your own momentum. I want to quote a poet on that situation – Walt Whitman:

"It is provided in the essence of things that from any fruition of success, no matter what, shall come forth something to make a greater struggle necessary."

That's a challenge which we can't get away from.

That's the challenge the proud history of Coca-Cola means to us. ...

You know there is a *feel* about this business. Some people don't get it. We are old enough and we must have the understanding to preserve in our policies the ideas and principles which our long experience has proved to be the solid foundation of our success. But hanging onto traditions will not do the job.

When I started here in 1923 I broke a lot of traditions. I preserved a number of them too. I wasn't too sure about some of the things we did. We can be more certain now, since we can look back and review them. What was good we must cling to. What I felt and thought I saw 24 years ago was a challenge and an opportunity to raise this business to a higher level.

The record speaks for itself. What I feel and see today, with more certainty and confidence than was within me in 1923, is a new challenge and a new opportunity to raise this business to a new and still higher level. Businesses which rest on their laurels are sleepy – will dry up and die.[23]

Even though Woodruff officially retired from the chairmanship of The Coca-Cola Company in 1955, he retained his influence on the company, through his position as chairman of the finance committee of the board, until his death on March 7, 1985, at the age of 95.

These three examples demonstrate that although the different phases in the lifecycle require different leadership roles, this doesn't necessarily imply that the different roles are embodied in different people, as it is possible for leaders to perform multiple roles for the same organization. However, this type of leader is probably the exception, it being more common for leaders to be more comfortable and effective in one particular leadership role. Some organizational lifestages, particularly the Creation and Turnaround phases, tend to be relatively short, and this would imply that leaders who focus on the Creator and Transformer roles tend to move from one organization to another. However, other lifestages, particularly the Maturity phase, can last a very long, even indefinite, time, and so you may see multiple Sustainers spending their entire careers at the same organization.

Notes

1. Ichbiah, Daniel, and Knepper, Susan L. 1991. *The Making of Microsoft: How Bill Gates and His Team Created the World's Most Successful Software Company*. Rocklin, CA: Prima Publishing, p. 21.
2. Ibid.
3. Microsoft. 2000. *Inside Out: Microsoft – In Our Own Words*. New York: Warner Books, p. 5.
4. Ibid, p. 72.
5. Ibid, p. 19.
6. Interview with David Frost, broadcast on Public Broadcasting Service, November 26, 1995.
7. Gore, Andrew. 2002. Pro File: Apple's Seeds. Q&A with Steve Wozniak. *MacWorld*, October, p. 23.
8. The Entrepreneur of the Decade: An Interview with Steve Jobs. *Inc*, April 1989, pp. 114–128, p. 118.
9. Wolf, Gary. 1996. Steve Jobs: The Next Insanely Great Thing. *Wired*, **4**(2): 102–163, p. 104.
10. Sheff, David. 1985. Interview with Steve Jobs. *Playboy Magazine*, February, p. 58.
11. Schlender, Brent. 1997. Something's Rotten in Cupertino. *Fortune*, March 3, pp. 101–8.
12. Booth, Cathy. 1997. Steve's Job: Restart Apple. *Time*, August 18, pp. 28–34. p. 31.
13. Steve Jobs' speech to MacWorld Expo, Boston, MA, August 13, 1997. Quoted from a transcript printed in *Computer Reseller News*, August 25, pp. 90–4.
14. Ibid.
15. Ibid.
16. Ibid.
17. Ibid.
18. Facts about the early history of The Coca-Cola Company are derived from two sources: Elliott, Charles. 1982. *"Mr. Anonymous" Robert W. Woodruff of Coca-Cola*. Atlanta: Cherokee; Pendergast, Mark. 1993. *For God, Country, and Coca-Cola. The Unauthorized History of the Great American Soft Drink and the Company that Makes It*. New York: Macmillan.
19. Elliott, Charles. 1982. *"Mr. Anonymous" Robert W. Woodruff of Coca-Cola*. Atlanta: Cherokee, p. 119.
20. Memo to the directors of The Coca-Cola Company, Robert W. Woodruff personal files, Special Collections and Archives, Robert W. Woodruff Library, Emory University.
21. See note 20, p. 126.
22. Remarks of R.W. Woodruff at fiftieth anniversary dinner, Coca-Cola Fountain Sales Corporation, Piedmont Driving Club, March 25, 1936. Robert W. Woodruff personal files, Special Collections and Archives, Robert W. Woodruff Library, Emory University.
23. Remarks of R.W. Woodruff at the Brookhaven Country Club, May 22, 1947. Robert W. Woodruff personal files, Special Collections and Archives, Robert W. Woodruff Library, Emory University.

CHAPTER 9

Case Study: The Walt Disney Company

Having developed the Leadership Lifecycle over the preceding chapters, including the leadership roles that correspond with the phases of the organization's lifecycle, the dangers inherent in transitions from one phase to another, and how it is possible for some individual leaders to span multiple roles, it is perhaps advantageous to illustrate the Lifecycle by looking at how the various roles and transitions apply over time within an organization. This chapter and the next will apply the model to two organizations that have enjoyed substantial and storied histories to provide a historical application of the Lifecycle to these respective organizations. This chapter applies the Lifecycle model to The Walt Disney Company, and the following chapter to Marks & Spencer.

The Creator Role

Walt Disney, like many of his creations, was a fairly simple character, but a person who had a strong vision and a passionate pursuit of that vision. One piece of Disney promotional literature described him as

> a very simple man – a quiet, pleasant man that you might not look twice at on the street. But a man – in the deepest sense of the term – with a mission. The mission is to bring happiness to millions.[1]

Walt's sense of mission and the passion he had for his characters – he was devastated when he lost control of his most popular early character, a rabbit named Oswald, to a distributor – made The Walt Disney Company what it was and would become. Although Walt was competent, he was not a talented illustrator – after the first early, rather crude beginnings, all the animation itself was done by others. But he was renowned for his story-telling ability, and the passion he would put into his characters, often acting out scenes to his illustrators, telling and retelling the stories to convey the sense of "aliveness" in his characters and the story that was being told.

Walt was first and foremost a Creator, constantly coming up with ideas which he would pursue with energy and passion. Once Walt was set on a project he was committed to the end and he would take great personal financial risks to explore new opportunities. For example, with his idea for the Disneyland theme park concept, his brother Roy, Disney's business manager, refused to fund Walt with the Walt Disney Studio's money, thinking it was a foolish plan. Nevertheless, Walt was determined to follow his idea and cashed in his life insurance, formed a new company, and attracted outside money to get the park off the ground.

Walt's passion and commitment to his ideas and visions bordered on obsession. For the parks he was just as much a storyteller as he was with his animated films, but with a different medium – concrete, wood, plastic and wires instead of film – to create a park not simply of rides, but of stories and fantasies that people could participate in, go through, be engaged by, and wonder at. His personal obsession led him to drive his designers and engineers as hard as he drove himself, but he drew a commitment to his mission that was strong and was to last beyond his life-time. This drive and work ethic, coupled with the same expectations for extraordinary performance from his followers, are common characteristics of Creators and often result, as it did for Walt, in a high level of commit-ment and effort from dedicated followers who share the same dream as the Creator. In his book *Prince of the Magic Kingdom*, Joe Flower describes this characteristic:[2]

> The energy and obsession that he poured into his projects are legendary within the Disney organization. As a child, he had always worked, whether milking the cows, selling newspapers on street corners, or taking photos of friends' children. As an adult, he rarely stopped working, arriving early and staying late, forced into taking vacations on doctors' orders more than once. He would regularly pay surprise visits to Disneyland, stand in line with the "guests", and take the rides himself, sometimes in the first car, sometimes in the last, looking for anything that might be out of place. The firehouse at Disneyland, near the train station on Main Street, has a small apartment upstairs. Disney would often spend the night there. In the morning the park workers would find notes scrib-bled on his distinctive blue paper stuck to their work places or in strategic spots around the park. The notes were instructions from "Walt": "Paint that curb",

"Move that bench", "Replace those flowers". He had been up during the night, roaming around the park, looking for ways to improve it.

Walt's natural gifts as a storyteller and his inventive, childlike imagination made him a naturally good communicator, enabling him to make a personal connection with others and inspire them with his vision, another valuable skill for a Creator. In fact, this was probably his biggest strength, enabling him to communicate the visions he had for animated films, other films, and the theme parks. Everything at Disney revolved around stories; even things as mundane as offices and studio lots were infused with stories and the attention to detail in these everyday tools reflected this obsession. The stories and Walt's ability to tell them was the "pixie dust" which gave energy to the organization.

For all the genius that was encapsulated in Walt Disney, he, like every entrepreneurial Creator, was subject to the whims of the external environment. And like most exceptional Creators, he was so compelled by his vision of how things should be that he wasn't perturbed by these outside influences and persisted in pursuing his vision despite any setbacks that came his way. Indeed, in the early years events seemed to be against Disney. He started making cartoon shorts and advertisements in Kansas City in 1920 with a partner called Ub Iwerks. By 1923 he had gone bankrupt. He left Kansas City for Hollywood and tried to become a film director – and failed. He then returned to cartoons, with Ub and his older brother Roy as business manager. He had early success with a rabbit named Oswald, but lost control of that to a distributor, forcing him to create a substitute, Mickey Mouse. After continued success with Mickey, and further character co-stars including Donald Duck, Pluto, and Goofy, he moved into expensive, risky, full-length animated features. The expense and lead-time involved in these movies, combined with the onset of World War II taking away much of his market, almost proved disastrous, and he barely escaped another bankruptcy.

However, environmental fortunes changed after the war was over. As soldiers returned from the war and economic stability and prosperity returned, the baby-boom generation was born, and the market for the type of family entertainment that Disney was producing boomed with the birth rate. This time, Walt Disney had the forces of the external environment in his favor in his ventures: the demographics of the population were right; the economy was burgeoning; the rest of the developed world was in turmoil after the war and looked to America to provide its needs. This was an opportunity seized by many American corporations to expand overseas, with any excess capacity from the domestic market eagerly gobbled up by consumer-good starved, war-torn nations. In this favorable environment, many American companies prospered, but especially Disney, as each element fell into place as if it were an imaginary fairy tale scripted by Walt himself.

Even beyond these demographic and economic blessings that were showered upon Disney, technology was also progressing quickly. Like a lot of Creators who see a vision of an improved future through changing technologies, Walt was always trying to be at the cutting edge, often inventing and developing the technology himself. In the early years, *Steamboat Willie*, Mickey Mouse's third film, was the world's first animated movie with synchronized sound – making Mickey an overnight worldwide success. Walt invented a multi-plane camera, which shot a picture through several planes of glass, each partially painted with elements of the foreground, enabling a three-dimensional effect to be created as cartoon characters walked through the scene. He experimented with color and sound, using the latest techniques as soon as they became available, and undertook daring subjects such as *Fantasia*. He developed a new kind of leisure place, far beyond the conventional fairground or amusement park. Disneyland would have attractions based on stories and characters that Disney made famous through his films, trying to capture people's imaginations and ignite a spark of Disney magic as they went through the park.

The Accelerator Role

While Walt Disney was undoubtedly a creative genius, and it was his ideas and stories that enabled Disney to come up with successive film successes and branch out into theme parks, Walt certainly did not have the financial and systems discipline that enabled Disney to succeed. So while Walt continued to lead the organization creatively, these elements of the Accelerator role were played by his brother Roy.

Although his only financial experience was as a bank teller, Roy provided the business acumen that Walt lacked and focused on growing the company within the bounds of growth that the company could afford. Playing this role while Walt, the flamboyant Creator, was still coming up with ever more fanciful and expensive projects proved particularly difficult and resulted in constant battles between them, even ending in them not speaking to each other for almost a decade.

The juxtaposition of Roy and Walt's roles at the growing Disney, and the resulting feud that ensued between them during the major growth phase of Disney, epitomizes the conflict between the Creator and Accelerator role and why it is rare for most Creators to successfully make the transition to the Accelerator role. Walt was the visionary Creator who was prepared to follow his vision, and take risks to do so, whatever the cost or investment required. The more successful he was, the larger the vision and projects became, and the bigger bets he would place to achieve them. Roy was the pragmatic Accelerator who wanted to grow the organization, but did not want to put the whole organization at risk for every successive project. Roy would seek to tone down the financial bets that the company took, and analyze the returns that the company would expect to achieve from these fanciful projects dreamed up by his younger brother. For instance, in the early 1950s, when Walt came up with the idea for a theme park to be based on Disney's characters, Disneyland, Roy was only prepared to venture $10,000 of the company's money to plan the project. Walt, however, determined to make Disneyland a fantasy-filled wonder, borrowed a further $100,000 against his life insurance policy to develop the project. Even in building the park, Roy lessened Disney's risk in the project by going outside the company for backers, with the company only taking an initial 34.48% equity slice of Disneyland when it opened, with Walt himself owning a further 17.25% for the stake he personally put up, but with the company buying back the rest from other backers within five years after the park had proved a success.

Despite, or perhaps because of, the constant conflict between Walt's continued Creation role and Roy's disciplined Accelerator role, the company was a phenomenal success. By 1966, the year of Walt's death, Walt Disney had received over 700 commendations, proclamations, awards, and medals from universities, societies, and governments. Hollywood had bestowed on him 29 Academy Awards for his films and four Emmys for his television shows. He was also one of the wealthiest men in the affluent entertainment industry, with the Disney family owning 34% of Walt Disney Productions, and Walt himself with an annual income well in excess of $2 million. Also, unlike any other Hollywood studio, Disney controlled every aspect of production and distribution of its output, and the name Disney was one of the best-known brand names in the world, synonymous with quality family entertainment.

The Sustainer Role

It was the combination of Walt's exuberance and Roy's rationality which enabled Disney to grow and prosper, such that when Walt died the company was on a sound financial footing, was growing at a fair pace, had acquired 28,000 acres in Florida to build more theme parks, and growth was being funded from current operations, leaving the company with very little debt on its books. However, without Walt's creative spark, Disney fossilized almost overnight, replacing Walt Disney the leader with Walt Disney the legend.

By achieving the performance that built Disney into a name synonymous with quality family entertainment, and Walt's continued focus on animated classics and new storytelling ideas such as Disneyland, and futuristic concepts such as his plan for EPCOT (the Experimental Prototype Community Of Tomorrow), Walt Disney was able to build a culture that continually fed into itself pursuing Walt's vision. However, after Walt's death, things changed. The stature of the man who had become the organization paralyzed that organization now that he was gone. Instead of the continued creative energy pushing the frontiers with new, unusual ideas that had kept Disney in the forefront, the organization closed in on itself, attempting to keep things the way they were when Walt was around. Flower describes this in two passages:

> Walt's organization and projects were now in the hands of men who were dedicated to his memory, ferocious in their desire to fulfill his dreams, competent, hard-working rational men who subjected every decision to the litany response, "What would Walt have done?" But they were not Walt. They did not have his peculiar madness. And without that peculiar madness, that "genius", things fell apart.[3]

> In a sense, Walt Disney's very success was his gravest failure. Although Walt Disney Productions was a large organization, with hundreds of creative animators, writers, designers, engineers, and architects, its personality was an extension of Walt Disney himself. Without him, the company was leaderless and, in some ways, brain dead. There was no one who could take his place. He had shaped the organization to meet his own needs. People ambitious enough to want recognition in the world had largely elected not to work in his shadow. The good news for Walt Disney Productions had been that Walt was an autocratic visionary capable of thinking grand new thoughts and pushing them into reality. The bad news, now that Walt was gone, was that the company consisted of people who were used to working for an autocratic visionary: they had been trained to expect the big ideas and the big decisions to come from the top. In Walt's absence many of them were not able to create anything on their own. The danger was that the company would fall back on rote, doing things the way they had been done before. As Randy Bright [one of the designers of EPCOT]

put it, "Walt left an organization that wasn't used to making decisions. It was used to saying, 'Well, Diz will tell us if this is right or not.'"[4]

Immediately after Walt's death, Roy took over as chairman of the company. However, as if to visibly illustrate the shift to the Sustainer role and Maturity phase that the company was entering into, Roy, realizing his lack of capacity on the creative side of the business, and seeking consensus as the organization moved forward, ran the company by committee. This included a committee at the top, firstly the "Disney Troika" consisting of Roy, Donn Tatum, who became president of the company, and Card Walker, who became executive vice president for operations. In addition, an executive committee was set up to run the organization that consisted of Roy, Tatum, and Walker, together with film producers Bill Anderson and Bill Walsh, Roy E. Disney Jr., and Walt's son-in-law Ron Miller. Although Roy was technically the head of the company, essentially these committees filled the Sustainer role and ran the organization.

Over the next few years, the organization essentially carried on, executing the projects that Walt already had underway, including the Walt Disney World theme park in Orlando, and eventually a scaled down version of Walt's vision for EPCOT. Less than three months after the opening of Walt Disney World in October 1971, Roy died, leaving Tatum and Walker to run the company. Tatum and Walker came from different sides of the company, Tatum was a "Roy man" from the financial side of the business, while Walker was a "Walt man" from the creative side. In time the organization itself became more and more polarized between "Walt men" and "Roy men," echoing the conflicts between Walt and Roy themselves, although this time not with such a productive outcome.

The Disney organization deteriorated into a closed organization with a growing amount of political and turf battles, to the point where politics became more important than productions. They stopped looking for new talent, or nurturing the talent they had. The pervading attitude emanating from the top was that it was a privilege to work at Disney, that talent will beat a path to Disney's door, and if it was good enough would go on and beat down the door in order to get in. Far from pursuing what Walt would truly have done, that is, continually seek new ideas and staying abreast, or preferably ahead, of new technological breakthroughs, the Disney organization tried to preserve Walt's dream by keeping things the way they were. This not only shut down openness to the creativity and new ideas that were the lifeblood of Disney, but also led over time to the ossification of the studio's technical abilities, which fell further and further behind the rest of the industry, as they continued to utilize the same movie-making equipment that Walt had used decades earlier, despite the subsequent technological advances.

All this resulted in a precipitous decline in Disney's performance. The only successful movie in the years after Walt's death was *The Love Bug* in 1969. However, even this success may have contributed to future disappointments, as it further reinforced the old Disney formula in the minds of the Disney executives long after the market had changed. It was only Disneyland and then, from 1971, Walt Disney World that kept the organization afloat, as the studio produced loss-maker after loss-maker.

In 1980, Tatum stepped aside and Walker became Chairman and CEO, and named his ally, Walt's son-in-law, Ron Miller as President and Chief Operating Officer. Miller, who had previously been head of production, concentrated his efforts on the studio side of the business, although creativity was not his strong suit. As even one of his admirers put it: "Ron Miller is a man who's extremely good-hearted and kind and did things for me that I'll never stop being grateful for. He is not a creative genius."[5] Thus, unsurprisingly, the studio continued to flounder. Yet, when Walker retired in 1983, shortly after he had succeeded in bringing Walt's final project, EPCOT, to life, he named Ron Miller as CEO over the objections of Roy Disney's son (and Walt's nephew), Roy E. Disney.

Along with disastrous performance at the box office came parallel financial effects. The studio's income had declined from $36.4 million in 1981 to $19.6 million in 1982, followed by a $33.3 million loss in 1983. The number of films the studio made dropped to three in 1983, and the portion of each film's cost represented by studio overhead climbed to 35%, far above the industry average of 20%. Even with the continued success of the parks, for the company overall, earnings per share slid to 75¢ in 1982 and to 68¢ in 1983 and did not seem to have prospects for recovering. The stock price fell by almost half in twelve months, from $84 per share in 1983 into the mid-$40s by early 1984.[6] The market value of the whole company was less than the value of just the parks. As if symbolizing how deeply Disney was troubled, there was even a strike at Disneyland.

The Transformer Role

In observing how companies in slow decline are able to recognize the need for a Transformer, frequently it takes a crisis to jolt the organization out of the mire. Disney was unquestionably in a potentially terminal spiral, and the crisis came in 1984.[7] For some time Saul Steinberg, Chairman of Reliance Group Holdings, a private investment company, had had his eye on Disney. He saw a seriously undervalued company with assets worth far more than what it would take to acquire the company, and that Disney was not making use of the assets they had – the vast landholdings in Florida, the films they had in their archives, and the characters they had developed. According to Steinberg:

> There was a lot of fuzzy thinking at Disney. They were very confused and financially naive. There was no leadership there. They were a company that was floundering. Walt Disney had the burning vision. Now he was gone and there wasn't anybody to take it the next series of steps. But it was an asset that couldn't be replaced. It could make an incredible amount of money.[8]

He, like most people outside the company, was also not exactly impressed with the management team:

> We had heard that this guy Ron Miller (the CEO of Disney) was not terribly competent. He was way in over his head. He used to play cards a lot. Maybe his head was into other things, I don't know. He was a football player at one time. He was described to us as a real dope. I don't know him personally, so I can't say. What he had done with the company was dopey and dumb.[9]

On Friday March 9, Steinberg heard the news that Roy Disney had resigned from the board and he interpreted that as a signal that Disney was about to be "put into play" as the terminology went on Wall Street. His reasoning was that Roy would only resign from the board of the company that bears his family name if he were about to bid for it himself, which he couldn't do while on the board. Steinberg's immediate reaction was to buy Disney stock as fast as he could.

Steinberg's interpretation was right, Roy was trying to form a group with enough power to reform Disney. But within weeks, Steinberg owned more Disney stock, 6.3%, than Roy Disney did. Despite buying in the market himself, Roy only owned 4.7%.

In response to this activity, Disney's management arranged an emergency $1.3 billion line of credit from the Bank of America in order to finance any defensive moves it might have to make and consulted with their investment bankers, Morgan Stanley.

By April 9, Steinberg owned 8.3% of Disney and on April 25 he made an official declaration that he intended to increase his holding to 25%. At the same time, Roy Disney was meeting with Michael Milken at Drexel Burnham Lambert to try to put together financing for a buyout of their own.

Meanwhile, The Walt Disney Company searched around for acquisitions in order to make the company less attractive to a takeover bidder, by diluting the stock and acquiring debt. They found one in Arvida, a Florida land-development firm owned by Bass Brothers Enterprises, a $4 billion conglomerate run by Sir Richardson Bass. Within days, Disney bought Arvida for a $200 million stock swap, for a company purchased by the Basses six months earlier with a $20 million cash investment, and which instantly made the Bass brothers among Disney's largest shareholders, along with Steinberg and Roy Disney.

On May 25, Steinberg sued Disney to prevent the Arvida acquisition, and simultaneously announced plans to purchase up to 49.9% of Disney. Four days later Steinberg announced a proxy fight to gain control of the company. Roy Disney tried to negotiate to buy the trademarks, the studio, and the merchandising for $350 million, leaving Steinberg the parks. Although it was obvious to everyone that if Steinberg won he would have to split the company up, thus ending the Walt Disney Corporation as a whole entity, Steinberg dismissed Roy's offer – he had already had an offer in hand from the owners of MGM/UA for $447 million for the studio alone.

Meanwhile Disney continued to search for acquisition candidates to act as "poison pills" – acquisitions that would make Disney unattractive to Steinberg and the other suitors. It agreed to acquire Gibson Greetings Cards for a combination of stock and cash – a deal worth between $300 and $400 million, for a company purchased only two years before for $1 million.

Steinberg's reaction was to step up the pace of the acquisition – to buy the whole of Disney before it could make another disastrous acquisition. On June 8, when the Disney stock was trading at $65 per share, Steinberg made a tender offer for Disney of $67.50 per share, or $71.50 per share if Disney dropped the Gibson deal.

Disney itself came up with a last-ditch strategy to fend off Steinberg: it would offer to buy him out, and at the same time make the alternative disastrous for Steinberg. It would, if Steinberg declined, make a "self-tender" offer to the other shareholders at a much higher price, thus leaving Steinberg with control of a company that was completely paralyzed with debt. It worked. Steinberg reluctantly realized that the Disney management was serious in its threat, and in the end Disney bought him out for a $32 million premium on his stock, plus another $28 million for his expenses.

However, this near-death experience was not the end of the threats to The Walt Disney Company. Steinberg's efforts had attracted attention to Disney, and now that Steinberg had inflicted the first wounds, others moved in for the kill. One of the buyers was Irwin Jacobs, a Minneapolis-based financier who bought and broke up companies, although generally on a smaller scale than Disney. However, by July 18, he was Disney's biggest shareholder. By this time, Roy Disney, whose resignation from the board had triggered the takeover frenzy in the first place, patched things up and rejoined the board, hoping to replace the management from within. Jacobs also felt a change in management was necessary, and both opposed the Gibson deal. Finally, on August 17, the board met and decided to back out of the Gibson deal, and formed a committee whose purpose was to replace the CEO, Ron Miller. Fortunately, Michael Eisner, the person the board and the major shareholders finally agreed to go after as the new CEO and potential Transformer for the organization, was dissatisfied and looking to leave his current studio, Paramount. He had been approached by Disney a couple of years before, but had refused to jump unless the top job was open. Now it was and, on September 22, 1984, he jumped.

The shareholders and board had agreed to the choice of Michael Eisner as the new CEO, and so Disney was snatched from the jaws of death and given a temporary respite – but Eisner was well aware that the honeymoon would be short. Frank Wells, an entertainment lawyer, former vice president of Warner's and a friend of the Basses, had also been brought in as part of the new management team, and Eisner rapidly coaxed Jeff Katzenberg, his protégé and former colleague at Paramount, to join him as head of Disney Studios.

A dramatic event, such as the hostile takeover attempt that Disney had just experienced, is often needed to provide the catalyst for a turnaround, jolting the organization into realizing that it is in potentially terminal decline, and paving the way for a Transformer to come in and rescue the organization. As part of the discussions leading to Eisner taking the job, and in his first few weeks on the job, he managed to persuade the major shareholders, and potential bidders for the company, that the organization was worth more together with him leading it than it was broken up, which both Steinberg and Jacobs would have been forced to do in order to reduce their debt burden that they would have had to take on to take over the company. Eisner was also aware of where Disney was in its lifecycle and how the natural tendencies of an organization in the Maturity phase had resulted in the position it was now in. In persuading Sid Bass, the single largest shareholder, that he was the person for the job, he contended:

> Companies like Disney are always founded by creative entrepreneurs, but eventually the founder dies or gets pushed out, or moves onto something else. Inevitably the businesspeople take over – the managers – and they focus on

preserving the vision that made the company great in the first place. They don't have any creative ideas themselves and they end up surrounding themselves instead with analysts and accountants to try to control the creative people and cut costs. In the process, they discourage change and new initiatives and reinvention. In time, the company begins to ossify and atrophy and die. It's important to have financial parameters and never bet the house, which is how we always protected Paramount. But in a creative business, you also have to be willing to take chances and even to fail sometimes, because otherwise nothing innovative is ever going to happen. If you're only comfortable running a business by the numbers, I can understand that. But then you shouldn't get involved with a creatively driven company like Disney.[10]

In this one statement, Eisner summed up how the lifecycle model operates, and applied it specifically to Disney. He also challenged Sid Bass to examine which part of the lifecycle he was comfortable in, as a Transformer was clearly needed at Disney and with that came a creative side as well as a required financial discipline. Bass was convinced and agreed to support Eisner for the job in what was probably the critical moment in securing the role for Eisner. Indeed, shortly after Eisner was appointed as CEO, the Bass brothers bought out the holdings of arbitrager Ivan Boesky and Jacobs, increasing their stake to 25% of the company and promising Eisner that they would not sell for at least five years, such was their confidence in Eisner's ability to turn Disney around.

Eisner, who had been described as "more hands on than Mother Theresa,"[11] quickly set about initiating change and, just as importantly, the appearance of change in the Disney organization. It was immediately apparent that he had a passion for Disney and would try and reawaken that passion in those that had seen their enthusiasm dwindle over the past years. It was also clear to Eisner that the organization had lost the passion, or the "magic" in Disney terms, and was becoming insular and arrogant. Eisner described the attitude at the parks:

> Our long run of success at the parks inevitably prompted management to become more ingrown and bureaucratic, more protective of the status quo and more arrogant. It was at the parks, in particular, that we felt we should do everything ourselves. We were the experts and no one could do it as well as we could.[12]

As a Transformer, Eisner needed to address the operational concerns that were plaguing Disney, as well as bringing back the vision to the organization which had been lost or dimmed at the end of the Maturity phase, causing the organization to go into decline. Eisner very clearly saw the need for Disney to recapture the vision of what Walt stood for, how this underlay the operational changes that were needed, and what his role was in bringing back that focus on the vision:

> Walt's genius had been to make Disney synonymous with the best in family entertainment – whether it was a theme park or a television show, an animated movie or even a Mickey Mouse watch. Customers did seek out Disney products, just as they were drawn to Disney animated movies, or visited Disney's Magic Kingdom. The name "Disney" promised a certain kind of experience: wholesome family fun appropriate for kids of any age, a high level of excellence in its products, and a predictable set of values. By the time Frank and I took over, nearly two decades after Walt's death, Disney had begun to seem awkward, old-fashioned, even a bit directionless. But that was misleading. The underlying qualities that made the company special lived on, just the way a person's character endures. Our job wasn't to create something new, but to bring back the magic.[13]

Together with the underlying vision of bringing back Walt's magic to the company, Eisner brought a relentless passion and energy in his pursuit of operational improvements. He held meetings or "gong-shows" with all the key people in the organization, even on Sunday mornings at his home, to try and assess how Disney could be turned around quickly. Eisner was hired as someone with the reputation for creativity, and he understood that creativity was the lifeblood of Disney – lifeblood that was being sucked dry by the old guard trying to hold on to the "What would Walt have done?" ethos. Eisner was determined to administer a rapid transfusion. The mission of Disney was to entertain and central to that were the "imaginers" – the creative heart of Disney. At one of his first meetings with the animation people, the people who had produced all the Disney classics, to discuss what projects they had in mind, even the creative "imaginers" were surprised by Eisner's creativity and enthusiasm. Far from constraining them, as the old management had done, it was apparent that they would be hard pressed to keep up with Eisner.

Along with the extensive internal communication through the "gong-shows" and the reputation for an exhaustive work ethic that spread like wildfire through the Disney organization, Eisner lost no time in broadcasting Disney's upcoming transformation to the world, announcing new rides for the parks based on *Star Wars* and *Raiders of the Lost Ark* in conjunction with George Lucas, and a project with Michael Jackson. Eisner also introduced the parks to something that they had never come across before – advertising. Disneyland's 30th birthday was in 1985, and Eisner was going to make it an event – every 30th guest would get a free pass, every 300th a stuffed toy, every 3,000th a Chevrolet, every 300,000th a Cadillac. The 250 millionth guest in Disneyland's history, due sometime in mid-summer, would get a Cadillac, 30,000 miles of air travel and 30 free visits to Disney parks.

This renewal of Disney under Eisner translated rapidly into improved financial performance with revenues up 22%, operating income up 44% and net profit up 77% in his first full year. Attendance at Disneyland went from 9.5 million in 1984 to 11.3 million in 1985, despite higher admission charges.

Still, Eisner was just beginning. Under the dual leadership of Eisner and Katzenberg, the studio side of Disney was also undergoing rapid transformation, and new areas such as the booming video industry were beginning to be exploited. Originally, under the old management, Disney had fought the introduction of video recorders in an attempt to protect the market value of movies it might show on the Disney Channel. But when the video manufacturers prevailed, the public embraced them and, with Disney under new management, Disney turned to the new medium, seeing it as an opportunity to exploit its library of classic films. In 1986, Disney sold 1.2 million copies of *Sleeping Beauty*; in 1987 it sold 3.2 million copies of *The Lady and the Tramp*. By 1987, of the 20 bestselling children's videos in the country, 18 were released by Disney, and in 1988 Disney sold 7.5 million copies of *Cinderella* and became number one in the entire home video industry.

In the studio, Katzenberg was making an equally dramatic impact. With *Three Men and a Baby* ($167 million in gross box office receipts), *Good Morning, Vietnam* ($124 million), and *Who Framed Roger Rabbit?* ($152 million), Disney became the first studio in history to release two films back-to-back – not to mention three in one year – which grossed over $100 million domestically. In the same year, 1988, *Cocktail* grossed $75 million, *Big Business* brought in $40 million and the re-release of *Bambi* brought in a further $38 million.

This was going on during the mid-1980s, the age of the yuppie, and in the midst of the biggest bull market the world has ever seen. It was boom time, a time of ostentation and conspicuous consumption, and nowhere was this more true than in Hollywood. Money flowed freely and expenses accordingly rose rapidly. The average production cost of a feature film in 1983 was under $12 million. By 1985 it was approaching $16 million, and by 1991, the average was $26.8 million, with "blockbuster" films regularly hitting the $50 million mark. But Disney took a more prudent approach, avoiding big name stars with equally headline grabbing fees, instead turning to young hopefuls and former stars who had slipped from Hollywood's all too brief limelight. However, even Disney could not altogether resist the spiraling costs. Its 1988 Spielberg hit *Who Framed Roger Rabbit?* cost over $50 million, and the 1990 movie *Dick Tracy*, even without paying star prices for Madonna, cost $47 million, with an additional $55 million in promotion costs.

However, Disney still managed to keep costs down relative to the rest of the industry, and the booming 1980s meant people had plenty to spend on entertainment – at the movies, on videos, and at the parks. The economy let Disney rapidly increase ticket prices at the parks without adversely affecting attendance. Ten price increases increased the adult ticket to Disneyland to $21.50 by 1988 and to $25.50 by 1990, with virtually all the extra revenue adding straight to the bottom line. Overall company revenues, which stood at $1.7 billion in 1984 before Eisner's arrival, hit almost $3 billion in 1987. Net income increased from $98 million to $445 million over the same period, with annual increases averaging over 50% and reaching 80% in 1987. Disney's return on equity rose from 8% when Eisner took over to 15% in 1985, 19% in 1986, and an incredible 27% in 1987. The stock price increased twelvefold from the mid-1980s to the beginning of the 1990s.

A Second Decline and Transformation

However, the successes of the latter half of the 1980s were difficult to sustain well into the 1990s. By 1994, with the tragic death of Frank Wells in a helicopter crash, the temporary absence of Eisner due to heart surgery, and a split with Jeffrey Katzenberg which resulted in him leaving the firm on acrimonious terms, the financial media was once again painting Disney as a troubled company. The successful turnaround of the last decade was also beginning to result in a heroic self-concept again manifesting itself throughout the organization. *Forbes* magazine even ventured that Disney was "overweight, arrogant, and paranoid."[14] A combination of macro-environmental effects such as a worldwide recession in the early 1990s, travel concerns due to the Gulf War, together with company-specific setbacks such as financial difficulties with the opening of the new European park outside Paris, and the creeping complacency which was beginning to invade the company once again meant that a decade after taking over Disney, Eisner was once again faced with the need to reinvigorate the company. As he put it:

When Frank [Wells] and I sat down to talk in my office late on Friday, March 25, 1994, we had reasons to feel both hopeful and concerned. Three weeks earlier, we'd finally concluded the Disneyland Paris financial restructuring that had occupied so much of our time and attention during the previous six months. There were undeniably more issues ahead. Attendance at the domestic parks remained flat, and Disney's performance in live action [movies] was still poor. We continued to be concerned about a growing blend of complacency and self-satisfaction, and a diminution of the passionate team spirit that marked the early years. No one was more openly restless than Jeffrey Katzenberg. Important as he had been to our success, Frank and I agreed that unless we could inspire Jeffrey to become a team player again, it might be necessary to part ways. What seemed clear was that the time had come to renew the company for a second time – to move some of our young executives around, to rethink our existing businesses, and to explore new ones, despite the short-term pain and dislocation such changes were likely to cause.[15]

Following the death of Frank Wells, the quest to fill his position led to two expensive failures in judgment. First, the matter of the departure of Katzenberg, when Eisner refused to name him as Wells' successor, ended up in court, with Eisner refusing to settle Katzenberg's contract which called for him to receive 2% of future revenues from projects that Katzenberg had initiated. The huge successes of, among others, *Beauty and the Beast* and particularly *The Lion King* left Katzenberg with a large claim, which he eventually won through the courts to the tune of $270 million, far higher than the $90 million he reportedly would have taken if Disney had settled at the time he left.[16] To find a successor to Frank Wells, Eisner wooed Hollywood star Michael Ovitz, founder of Creative Artists Agency, and considered one of the most powerful men in Hollywood, to come to Disney as his number two executive. After lengthy negotiations, Eisner succeeded in luring Ovitz to Disney. It was a disaster from the start. Not only did Ovitz's arrival prompt other senior Disney executives to leave after finding him impossible to work with, but Ovitz, the consummate dealmaker, remained focused on deal-making, whereas Eisner was hoping that he would take some of the operating burden away from him. Instead, Eisner had to be even more involved in operations, doing those things that Ovitz left undone, and undoing those that he did. For Ovitz's part, he commented:

[Eisner] was my best friend for 25 years. To this day I don't know why he brought me in there. ... He was supposed to be less hands-on. He says I didn't know what I was doing, but he didn't give me the opportunity to do anything. We were going to be partners. We were going to run the company together. He brought me in as his successor. I thought there would be a two- or three-year learning curve. But it didn't work from the day I started.[17]

Less than a year and a half after bringing Ovitz to Disney, Eisner let him go with a departing package of cash and stock options worth more than $90 million.[18]

Operationally, Eisner set about shaking Disney out of its slump by investment in new projects and a major acquisition, but achieved only mixed results. On the theme park side Eisner had several projects in mind, the most radical of which was Disney's America, a historically based theme park to be located in Virginia. After a lot of planning, the public announcement of the park caused a public uproar and vehement objections to the park, and particularly the site, and eventually the plan was dropped. In California, Eisner wanted to expand the Disneyland site, and the dropping of Disney's America concept led to an adaptation of the theme, which became realized as Disney's California Adventure, which opened in 2001. In Orlando, another new theme park was developed, Animal Kingdom, a departure from the concept of totally controlled environment as it contained live animals, but was an instant hit from the day it opened in April 1998. In Orlando, Disney also introduced its Wide World of Sports complex, the Disney Institute, which combined learning and vacation, and even built its own town, Celebration, which was closer to Walt's original dream for EPCOT as an actual place for people to live in an idealized environment.

On the studio side, a shift was made to a potentially riskier strategy to focus on producing blockbuster, star-driven movies which would appeal to a larger international audience. This strategy brought initial success with several big hits in the first couple of years such as *Phenomenon*, *The Rock*, a live-action version of *101 Dalmatians*, *Ransom*, and *Armageddon*. On the animation side, Disney partnered with Pixar who specialized in computer-animated movies to produce the first entirely computer-animated movie, *Toy Story*, which was an enormous success, and was followed by *A Bug's Life*, *Toy Story 2*, and *Monsters, Inc.*, all of which were hits at the box office and on home video. Added to the line-up were Disney's own new animated movies, *Pocahontas*, *The Hunchback of Notre Dame*, *Hercules*, *Mulan*, *Tarzan*, *Fantasia 2000*, *Atlantis*, and *Lilo and Stitch*. However, while each was profitable, none scaled the high expectations previously set by *The Lion King*. Disney also ventured successfully into a new arena for animation – films released directly to video without a theatrical presentation. These films were a lot less expensively produced, yet managed to draw critical acclaim and generate substantial profits.

By far the biggest move Eisner made, however, was the acquisition of Cap Cities/ABC, which not only provided Disney with one of the big three networks, but also additional cable channels, most notably the leading sports channel, ESPN. Eisner saw the acquisition of a network as essential to Disney to guarantee an outlet for its television production, as the networks were increasingly moving towards providing their own content. Additionally, Eisner saw television exposure for the Disney brand and characters as a synergistic endeavor spilling over positive benefits to the theme parks and movie business. So after making overtures and negotiating at various times with all three networks, Disney acquired Cap Cities/ABC in the summer of 1995. While the acquisition of ABC certainly guaranteed the distribution outlet for Disney's output, and there were other synergies such as using the ESPN brand within the parks and developing stores and restaurants such as ESPN Zone to further Disney's reach, the acquisition was not without problems. The biggest of these was the core ABC network, which was the number one network when Disney bought it, yet suffered a rapid decline in its prime-time audience in the seasons following the purchase. Even Disney's injection of content into areas such as children's programming on Saturday mornings could not offset the fall in ABC's overall ratings which slipped to the bottom of the major networks.

Where Does Disney Go from Here?

At the time of writing in mid-2002, Disney once again seems to be at a transition point. Media reports have once again started citing Disney's decline or at least major difficulties, and again hold out the specter of a possible takeover as its stock languishes. Disney jumped on the internet bandwagon and made huge investments in the internet, buying Starwave and Infoseek and investing in the Disney Go network, which combined lost hundreds of millions of dollars and forced large write-offs on the income statement and balance sheet. The terrorist attack of September 11 2001 had an enormous impact on most of Disney's business, but particularly the theme parks where attendance declined precipitously, and the continued threat of further terrorism, together with a general economic recession, continues to dampen park attendance. ABC continues to struggle, and Disney has suffered from a high turnover at the top of ABC, going through five presidents of the division in as many years, yet failing to revive the prime-time ratings in any sustained way. ABC continues to try new shows, debuting more new series than any other network, yet failing to come up with the two or three successful shows that can drive the ratings, while in the meantime having to give away free time to advertisers to make up for poor ratings in previous seasons.

The question is, can Eisner continue to spark the creative energy of Disney, and maintain focus on the mission, without it developing into a corporate monolith, insensitive to the public it has delighted for so long, which is hinted at by some of its recent actions? In her recent critical book on Eisner, *The Keys to the Kingdom: How Michael Eisner Lost His Grip*, Kim Masters characterizes Eisner as an "increasingly isolated and Nixonian executive" and poses the question "Was Eisner the man to lead Disney into the twenty-first century or was he too controlling, too arrogant, and simply too unedited to work the old magic?"[19] After years of being the highest paid executive in America, the roller-coaster ride at Disney, the death of his counterpart and friend Frank Wells, and his own heart problems, Eisner has to prove himself again and demonstrate that he still has the energy and passion to revive Disney once again. As Eisner himself wrote to novelist Larry McMurtry, in response to McMurtry's letter describing his own heart surgery and his sense of emptiness following the surgery:

> Something has happened to me that is a big deal. I am no longer immortal. I am no longer even young. … I still go to the office and still am basically the same person, but there is this giant hole which I guess is called middle age. Or actually is old age … 52 is half of 104 and therefore 52 is not middle age. 52 for me is old age. That's the rub. … I went from a kid to old age in four hours. …

> I do not like what has happened, but I guess it's better than many I know. I don't have cancer or any other horrible illness that I know about. But I am different. My life has a finite sense to it, and there is certainly a hollowness that comes with such realizations. I try not to think about it, but I think about it all the time. … I work as I worked before, but I know it isn't as important as it was before.[20]

Only time will tell if Eisner is willing and able to work his magic once more, or whether Disney slips into a state of heroic self-concept, followed by the inevitable dysfunctional performance which will force Disney once again to face the threat of takeover or await another savior.

Notes

1. Flower, Joe. 1991. *Prince of the Magic Kingdom: Michael Eisner and the Re-making of Disney*. New York: John Wiley & Sons, p. 21.
2. Ibid, p. 25.
3. Ibid, p. 53.

4. Ibid, p. 50.
5. Ibid, p. 59.
6. Ibid, pp. 96–7.
7. A full account of the takeover battle for The Walt Disney Company is given in: Taylor, John. 1987. *Storming the Magic Kingdom: Wall Street, The Raiders, and the Battle for Disney.* New York: Alfred A. Knopf.
8. See note 1, p. 101.
9. Ibid.
10. Eisner, Michael, with Schwartz, Tony. 1998. *Work in Progress.* New York: Random House pp.136–7.
11. Ibid, p. 143.
12. See note 10, p. 229.
13. Ibid, p. 235.
14. Koselka, Rita. 1991. Mickey's Midlife Crisis. *Forbes*, May 13, pp. 42–3.
15. See note 10, p. 293.
16. Masters, Kim. 2000. *The Keys to the Kingdom: How Michael Eisner Lost his Grip.* New York: HarperCollins.
17. Slater, Robert. 1997. *Ovitz.* New York: McGraw-Hill.
18. See note 16.
19. Ibid, p. 446.
20. See note 10, p. 350.

CHAPTER 10

Case Study: Marks & Spencer

Creator: Michael Marks

In 1882, a young Michael Marks fled the anti-Semitic pogroms in Russia which followed the 1881 assassination of Tsar Alexander II. Arriving in northern England, Michael went in search of work, seeking a tailoring factory that he had been told employed many immigrant Russian Jews. While trying to find this factory, he met Isaac Dewhirst, who had built up a modest wholesale business in Leeds. The two young men clicked instantly and Isaac invited Michael back to his warehouse, where, discovering that Michael had been a street seller back in Russia, he offered him five pounds in order to start a business selling goods in Leeds and the surrounding towns. Thus the quest for funding and for speed to market that often plagues Creators was instantly solved for Michael by this fortuitous meeting. However, the drive, determination, and passion of the Creator certainly wasn't lacking in the young Michael Marks.

Setting up initially only on a tray, from which he could sell his limited goods, Marks plied his trade well, despite his lack of mastery of the English language. Ironically, this impediment actually helped his business, as his inability to haggle in his customers' language prompted him to attach a sign to his tray which read "Don't ask the price, it's a penny," which had the effect of cutting out much of the profit-reducing haggling, a routine part of the street seller trade in that era.

Marks' salesmanship and perseverance soon enabled him to rent a trestle table at the local market, and then a stall in the covered market. This rapid progression, despite his language limitation, demonstrates traits and behaviors needed by the Creator. While little detail is known of his early beginnings, he was obviously a good salesman, and astute at under-standing the needs of his customers, having only the space for a very

limited number of goods on his stall. He was certainly passionate, ener-
getic and devoted to his business. Indeed, his son Simon recalled from his
childhood that his father "was, of course, pre-occupied with the building
up of his business to which he devoted all of his energies."[1]

As his trade progressed, he formed a friendship with the cashier at his
primary supplier, Dewhirst's, a young man named Tom Spencer. Meanwhile, Michael continued to expand his business, employing people to run
stalls for him so that he could set up shop in more than one town on the
same day. When he moved from the outdoor market to the indoor market
in Leeds, the sign above the stall read "M. Marks: the original Penny
Bazaar," soon shortened to "Marks Penny Bazaar."

As business continued to grow, Marks needed to supplement his own
skills as a Creator with those of an Accelerator in order to manage the
rapid growth that his enterprise was experiencing. In September 1894,
Tom Spencer invested his life savings of £300 into buying a half-share in
Michael Marks' penny bazaars, bringing with him his accountant's eyes
for meticulous detail and structure to complement Michael's passion and
energy. The creation of the partnership enabled them to open their first
actual store where the sign read "Marks & Spencer Penny Bazaar." The
structure brought to the partnership by Tom Spencer enabled the company
to grow rapidly in the coming decade, and by 1903, there were 36 Marks
& Spencer market bazaars and stores, including three in London. In 1905
Tom Spencer retired from the business, leaving Marks once again to run
the growing company. Unfortunately, however, 1907 saw the death both of
Tom Spencer and, within a few months, Michael Marks, who collapsed on
the way to visit one of his stores. By that time, the number of Marks &
Spencer outlets had reached 60, two-thirds of them stores, the rest estab-
lished penny bazaars in covered markets.

Accelerator: Simon Marks

Simon Marks, Michael's son, at age 19 had officially joined Marks &
Spencer just two months before his father's untimely death. Although he
had been brought up in the belief that he would one day take over the
family business, that day arrived sooner than he expected. However,
Marks & Spencer was firmly in the growth stage of the lifecycle at this
point, and Simon readily took on the leadership role of Accelerator,
putting systems in place that enabled the company to continue its rapid
growth. A trip to the United States to examine retail operations there
confirmed many of his own thoughts and ideas:

I learned the value of checking lists to control stocks and sales. I learned that new accounting machines could help to reduce the time formidably to give the necessary information in hours instead of weeks. I learned the value of counter footage and how, in the chain store operation, each foot of counter space had to pay wages, rent, overhead expenses and profit. There could be no blind spots in so far as goods are concerned. This meant a much more exhaustive study of the goods we were selling and the needs of the public. It meant that the staff who were operating had to be re-educated and retrained.[2]

His introduction of a management information system, or "checking lists" as he referred to them, had a dramatic impact on the business, enabling managers to have information on stocks and sales every two weeks instead of every quarter. Indeed, so efficient were the systems that Simon introduced early in his tenure that essentially the same systems remained in operation for 60 years, before finally being replaced with computerized systems in the early 1980s.

As well as putting systems in place to allow for growth, one of the tasks of the Accelerator is to build the brand and reputation of the organization. Early on, Simon focused on quality and value as the core attributes around which to build the reputation and brand. As one retired executive put it: "Quality and value became the lifeblood of Marks & Spencer and Simon was its beating heart."[3] Simon himself noted in his *Notes on the Business*, printed in 1954: "We are earning a reputation for good value and good taste. We must continue to deserve that reputation by avoiding garish and tawdry merchandise … An inexpensive item need not be shoddy."[4] As for a brand, Simon sanctified his father's name by creating the St Michael brand for Marks & Spencer products that would come to symbolize quality and value for 70 years. In creating the St Michael brand, Simon was fanatical about maintaining the quality of the goods sold under the St Michael name, instinctively realizing that the reputation of the whole business depended on maintaining the combination of quality and value, and refusing to have anything in the stores which did not live up to these standards, even if they sold well. Indeed, such was the focus on maintaining the consistency of the brand that until recently nobody inside the company would refer to St Michael as a brand at all, but referred to it instead as "the business."

Growth continued at a rapid pace for Marks & Spencer under Simon Marks. By 1927, the company had 135 stores and employed nearly 10,000 people. In 1926 the company had its initial public offering on the London Stock Exchange, returning for further rounds to keep pace with its growth in 1929, 1930 and 1934. Even during the hard years of the Depression of the 1930s, such was the quality and value represented by Marks & Spencer that the company kept growing despite the surrounding economy. Sales rose by a factor of ten from £2.4 million in 1929 to £23.4 million in 1939 with profits rising from £0.24 million in 1929, breaking the £1 million for the first time in 1935 to £1.7 million in 1939. By the outbreak of World War II in 1939, the company had 234 stores employing 17,000 people.

The war years curtailed the growth of the company, with efforts diverted to the war effort, including the use of the Marks & Spencer's headquarters by the government's clandestine Special Operations Executive and a role as an exporter to the United States, generating dollars for the war effort. Indeed, the Marks & Spencer Export Corporation generated over £10 million for the government during the course of the war. The company also saw more than 100 of its stores damaged by bombing and 16 completely destroyed. However, following the war, growth picked up as if uninterrupted, and although it took until 1957 to repair and rebuild all the damaged stores, by that time, sales had easily broken through £100 million a year.

One of the qualities of leadership which cuts across all the leadership roles at different stages of the organization's lifecycle is the willingness to adapt and change as the prevailing environment shifts and competition arises. One such example for Simon was the growth in Britain of the American chain F.W. Woolworth which was beginning to beat Marks & Spencer on its home turf. At one point, one of his store managers reported to him that two Woolworth's directors had been into a Marks & Spencer store and criticized some items as "lemons." While upset by this incident, Simon was willing enough to realize that the criticism was justified and to make changes to his stores. He remarked later: "I was afraid. And the question of how to react, what to do, was my concern day and night."[5] His solution was to not try to go head-to-head with Woolworth and create a price war that Marks and Spencer might lose, but to outflank his competition and differentiate Marks & Spencer by branching out into clothing, which soon became the dominant part of Marks & Spencer's business.

A further example of Simon's willingness to adapt and change was his "Operation Simplification" in the mid-1950s. Following the post-war growth of the company, Simon felt that it had become bloated and less efficient than it should be. Although the main role of the Accelerator is to put systems in place to allow for growth, as growth occurs, some of these systems themselves are outgrown and need to be discarded and replaced. Such was the mission of "Operation Simplification," which rid the company of many routines and procedures which had become outdated, and fundamentally restructured the business. An estimated 18 million forms were scrapped, saving 80 tonnes of paper a year and cutting some £4 million of overhead over two years.[6]

Within any of the leadership roles, different individual leaders can adopt different leadership styles with which to accomplish the role, although some styles may be more suited to certain roles than others. For example, whether or not the leader's decision-making style is autocratic or participative can vary within any particular role. However, an autocratic style is more often suitable in a Creator or Transformer role than in a Sustainer role, as the Creator and Transformer have to set a unique vision for the company and make some fundamental strategic choices for the direction of the company which may go against the wishes of others involved in the organization. However, in the Sustainer role, buy-in from others in the organization becomes more important as the strategic nature of the decisions is less a matter of life or death for the organization, and effective implementation requiring the cooperation of others becomes more important, thus generally being more compatible with a participative leadership style rather than an autocratic style. For the Accelerator, a strong case for either style could be made. Initially in the Growth phase, an autocratic style can be effective at overcoming the chaotic nature of the organization left by the Creator, imposing efficient systems and routines on the organization. Later on, a participative style could enable the organization to be more responsive to needed changes in the organizational systems by being more involved in monitoring the competitive environment. Simon Marks was clearly an autocrat. One former director recalled that:

> Simon was a monster. He ran the company as a total autocrat and was proud of it. "Give me no pro-consuls," he would say. Disagreeing with him could end your career. One chief accountant mildly pointed out what he saw as some flaws in Simon's thinking on a minor issue and was promptly fired.[7]

This referred to an incident in 1945 when the unfortunate Mr. J.H. Nellist, chief accountant, dared to disagree with the chairman. Simon had been telling him about a new plan when Nellist reputedly said: "I am concerned that might damage the business." Simon is reported as replying, "Well, if it does, you won't be around to see it."[8]

Simon's autocratic style was in some ways an outpouring of his passion for the business. He took everything personally and was involved in every aspect of the business. "There is nothing relating to Marks & Spencer that does not interest me,"[9] he would say. He would personally inspect every new line of garments and was ruthless if they didn't meet the quality or value standards he had set, berating selectors who had chosen substandard garments with "Why are you trying to ruin my business?"[10] While this style was natural for Simon, and worked well in building and protecting the ethos of quality and value in the culture of the company, it also fostered a culture of fearful obedience to an all-powerful chairman, which continued past Marks to subsequent holders of the chairman position and eventually led to the decline of the company.

Just as his father's sudden death at work had thrust Simon into the leadership role at Marks & Spencer, his own sudden death on December 8, 1964, also at work, marked the next leadership transition at the company. Characteristically, Simon had been inspecting garments and hurling them on the floor when they displeased him, berating their selectors with "You are trying to ruin my business," when he stormed out and collapsed with a massive heart attack.

As we saw in the previous chapter on The Walt Disney Company, the company became fossilized at the moment of Walt's death, as if preserving an imprint of the character of the leader. It is both a tribute and a condemnation of a forceful leader that nothing changes after the leader departs. In one respect, Simon Marks left behind a well-oiled machine that kept growing for so long under the value system that he left behind, based on the twin pillars of quality and value. On the other hand, because of the great success of the business under his leadership, nobody would dare attempt to change the way things were done for a very long time, and there was no bold or creative force left behind to push the company into new directions, but merely to run the business as Simon would have done.

The passing of Simon Marks and the transition to his successor, Israel Sieff, also marked the transition of the leadership role in the company from Accelerator to Sustainer.

Sustainer: Israel Sieff (Chairman, 1964–67)

Israel Sieff and Simon Marks had been friends since their teenage years when Israel met and started dating Simon's sister, Becky. The families became thoroughly intertwined when Israel married Becky, and later Simon married Israel's sister, Miriam. Although he had his own family business to attend to, Israel, a board member of Marks & Spencer at the time, joined Simon full time in the business when, in 1926, following a board meeting, Simon complained to Israel: "I have nobody to talk to. I'm surrounded by a bunch of morons." Israel replied, "Well that's all right. I'll join you for six months and sit in the next room so that you will have somebody to talk to." So on the first day of the General Strike of 1926,

Israel joined Simon at Marks & Spencer. However, instead of getting the office next to Simon's, Simon installed Israel's desk in his own office right next to his. Israel protested: "I wanted to go in the next room, because if I'm in the same room I'll only bother you with questions." To which Simon replied: "You must be in here because I want you to ask me questions. That's exactly what I want."[11]

Six months became 38 years as Israel continued to serve as Simon's right-hand man up until Simon's death, and was then himself named chairman of the company. Given the strong association and friendship that Israel had with Simon and the role he played as second-fiddle to Simon's leading role, it is unsurprising that he would continue to try and keep the company running as Simon had. In his memoirs, penned two decades after Simon's death, he wrote: "While he was alive he dominated me. I always deferred to him; it never occurred to me to do anything else. I grew up in the assumption of his superiority, as a brain, as a business leader and as a human being."[12]

Israel remained chairman of Marks & Spencer for three years after Simon's death, before handing over the mantle of chairman to his younger brother Edward, or Teddy Sieff. Israel's tenure is fairly typical of someone taking on the first, transitional Sustainer role after a long-tenured Creator or Accelerator has dominated the organization for an extended period. Much of Israel's role was in preparing the organization for the long haul, stabilizing the organization after the dynamism of his predecessor and attempting to democratize the organization following the autocratic reign of his predecessor. Israel was known and remembered for his attention to and care of the employees of the company, for promoting good human relations both within the organization and between the company and its suppliers, and for democratizing the ownership by giving all shareholders full voting rights, which had been denied by Simon, who essentially controlled the majority of voting rights.

Sustainer: Teddy Sieff (Chairman, 1967–72)

After Simon's death, the rigid hierarchical structure became more entrenched and internal politics grew in its importance and impact on the company. Through the reigns of Israel, Teddy, and Marcus Sieff, politics became rife in the organization. Executives were very conscious of status and the outward symbols of rank. Seniority was visible to everyone just by looking at the executive's office: how many windows it had, how big the desk was, how deep the pile of the carpet, the fabric of the curtains, how many armchairs there were, and the size of the secretary's office all clearly conveyed the importance of the executive in the organization.

The success of the organization and the centralized power structure enabled those at the top to live lives of absolute luxury. Directors entered the building by a discreet entrance at the back, they always traveled first-class on trains and planes and through the 1960s had chauffer-driven Rolls-Royces or Bentleys at their disposal. Jaguars took their place in the 1970s, with the exception of the chairman's car, and later Mercedes as Jaguars became less reliable. The directors from the founding family, who were still major shareholders, came to believe that a luxurious lifestyle both inside and outside the office was their proprietorial right and the culture of extravagance was easily adopted by the non-family directors as they joined the board. While Sustainers usually adopt a more participative leadership style appropriate for a mature organization, the opposite was true at Marks & Spencer where the chairman remained the ultimate source of autocratic authority. In time, the combination of the luxurious lifestyle and autocratic rule left the organization out of touch with its customers and the changing reality of the marketplace, and the seeds of complacency and decline were beginning to be sown, although it would still be some years before they grew to manifest themselves for all to see.

Sustainer: Marcus Sieff (Chairman, 1972–84)

One of the challenges which Sustainers face is how to maintain or revitalize the growth of an organization when the core business has reached a natural saturation point. Whereas Israel and Teddy had continued to follow Simon's philosophy of internal growth, Marcus broke with this tradition and began to look for growth by acquisition. The choice at this point in the lifecycle when growth in the core market has tapered off is to find a new market for the company's product, or expand the product offering. Marcus chose to expand the company's market geographically by acquiring People's Department Stores of Canada in 1974. By the end of Marcus's chairmanship, the company would have 227 stores in Canada, compared with 265 in its core UK market. However, with hindsight, Marcus paid too much for the acquisition, and the company was never able to make a success of the stores, resulting in an overall drag on company profitability. Additionally, with Marcus's focus on overseas expansion, there was a feeling in the organization that domestic growth was being neglected and that Sieff was content with positioning Marks & Spencer as an unassailable national institution rather than aggressively growing the organization, and profitability seemed to take a back seat to other priorities such as promoting the British textile industry and gaining political influence.

A primary cause of decline for organizations that have sustained success for a prolonged period is that it is the ways of achieving the ends, the processes, which become entrenched and valued as much as the ends themselves. The common cry of "but we've always done it this way" is heard as a reason to not change even when the circumstances or environment have changed. Indeed, it can be the very success of the processes themselves that can cause their failure. A good example of this is the relationship that Marks & Spencer had with its suppliers. Having joined the company shortly after World War II, Marcus Sieff was very concerned about sourcing as much of Marks & Spencer's merchandise as possible from within the UK, in order for M&S to play its part in growing employment and rebuilding the economy. He also felt that using domestic suppliers increased its flexibility in responding to changing fashions and allowed Marks & Spencer more control over maintaining the quality of the goods it sold. Indeed, this policy worked well for a long time. Over time, however, the UK textile industry went into decline due to overseas competition, resulting in a situation whereby Marks & Spencer's suppliers found themselves in an effective monopoly position as their domestic competition had vanished and M&S refused to contemplate sourcing abroad due to its long-held faith in Marcus Sieff's policy of sourcing from the UK. This led to complacency on the part of suppliers, and higher costs for Marks and Spencer, enabling competitors to grow at M&S's expense while its suppliers survived, protected from the same competition that M&S itself was facing.

Sustainer: Derek Rayner (Chairman, 1984–91)

Derek Rayner became the first non-family chairman of Marks & Spencer in 1984, after 102 years of family control. While this was a significant milestone in the company's history, and Rayner intended to bring some sweeping changes into the organization, he certainly wasn't an outsider and had no intention of changing the underlying vision of the organization, or disrupting the course set by the prior family chairmen. Indeed, Richard Greenbury, Rayner's successor, said of the move to a non-family chairman:

> Derek and I had been brought up by the family. They took us under their wing and developed us. And although we were not family, we were the nearest

thing. We both believed in the principles by which Simon had grown the business and Marcus and Teddy ran it – we believed those principles were fundamental to its success. Therefore although Derek and I modernized them – the attitude to people, to suppliers, to customers – we stuck to them so there was real continuity.[13]

On the day he took office, Rayner gathered the directors and senior officers together and outlined his six priorities for his chairmanship: internationalize the business, refurbish the stores, expand financial services, expand the food business, expand the selling space in the UK, and improve processes such as information systems, warehousing, and transportation.

One thing that didn't change under Rayner was that the organization remained effectively a dictatorship under the rule of the chairman. However, in the levels below the chairman, now that it was evident that you didn't have to be a family member to reach the top of the organization, the political maneuverings and concern with status became even more fierce as people positioned themselves for advancement. Stuart Rose, who was an executive under Marcus Sieff and Rayner, and who went on to become CEO of rival retail group Arcadia, commented:

> Under Marcus it was a benign dictatorship. He would shout at you but then he'd put his arm round you and say: "I'm only trying to teach you boy." Derek started to squeeze the business for profit and the organization became more political. You always had to mind your back.[14]

One of the Sieff family members also added:

> We felt things did begin to change under Derek. He kept the values but managers became more competitive and status conscious with each other, and it became almost a disadvantage to be a family member.[15]

Thus, while Rayner was able to institute some changes in the organization in line with his six priorities, with the result that profits more than doubled during his tenure, the upper levels of the organization were increasingly succumbing to a developing heroic self-concept, and the politics of the organization were becoming increasingly dysfunctional. However, while this was not felt in the bottom line during the booming 1980s, the boom times were also seeing the birth of increased competition in Marks & Spencer's mid-market clothing niche, with the result that competitive threats were beginning to increase.

Meanwhile, Rayner also had the desire to expand overseas, and his particular ambition was the United States, resulting in the purchase in 1988 of the venerable Brooks Brothers menswear chain for $750 million. Once again, however, this expansion overseas proved to be a folly for Marks & Spencer as it tightly managed an established retailer despite having little feel for the local market, resulting in the underperformance of its acquisition, which, despite added investment, it eventually sold in 2001 for $225 million; $525 million less than it had paid for it.

Sustainer: Richard Greenbury (Chairman, 1991–99)

Like the Sustainers who immediately followed Walt Disney at the company that bears his name, Richard Greenbury was described as "an innately cautious man whose idea of running Marks & Spencer was to think what Simon Marks would have done – and to try and interpret that into modern-day practice."[16] For Greenbury, this meant shying away from what he termed "acquisition retailing,"[17] and focusing on organic growth in the mode of his mentor Simon Marks and getting back to the fundamental operations of retailing. However, with this came what some saw as a lack of innovation and change. As one director put it: "Rick was a brilliant operational retailer but he couldn't innovate his way out of a paper bag."[18] Still operating in the dictatorial style of past Marks & Spencer chairmen, Greenbury was ruthless and paid little attention to the thoughts of others. As one store manager put it: "The place was ruled by fear."[19] Although Greenbury held longer board meetings than Rayner, preferring to launch a discussion on the strategies of the company rather than just stating them, the reality remained that strategy was being dictated solely by the chairman, as others were afraid to make their opinion known in case it conflicted with Greenbury's. While Greenbury's focus on the stores and the relationships with suppliers provided an initial boost to the company following the recession of the early 1990s, indeed reaching record profits of over £1 billion in 1997 and 1998, Greenbury's style eventually proved destructive to the company. As one non-executive director put it: "Most successful retailers are run by gifted dictators, and Rick was a dictator. The problem came when, after years of success, the company began to operate only to please Rick, not the customer."[20]

This lack of attention to the opinions of others extended to the company's relationships with the City, as Greenbury continued to ignore analysts and had little regard for shareholders. While the company could perhaps afford this aloofness while they continued to perform well, when the company's performance began slipping after its 1998 peak, they quickly found that they had no friends in the City and the financial markets were quick to punish the stock. One analyst commented:

> Their main problem with the City was that they didn't have any friends. They were arrogant, pompous and unworldly. They were in-turned and secretive with no network of outside supporters apart from suppliers. So when it rained they had no friends because it never occurred to them it might rain.[21]

The political atmosphere which had been growing within Marks & Spencer, and particularly among the senior officers, only intensified under Greenbury. Aware of the fact that there was no obvious successor, Greenbury, early in his tenure, set up a situation where the four potential successors were named as joint managing directors. This arrangement led to a increasingly tense situation, with each building support for themselves within the organization to the detriment of their attention on the business itself. Indeed, the political turmoil peaked in 1998 when one of the four joint managing directors, Keith Oates, attempted a boardroom coup to oust Greenbury. Although unsuccessful, and resulting in Oates' departure from the company, it was an unprecedented occurrence at Marks & Spencer and reflected the vulnerability of Greenbury's position and the political atmosphere within the upper echelons of the organization. Indeed, within a month, Greenbury appointed Peter Salsbury, one of the other joint managing directors, as chief executive under Greenbury's chairmanship and six months later, following an almost 50% collapse in profits for the year to May 1999, Greenbury resigned.

While each of the five men who led Marks & Spencer in the Sustainer role had slightly different emphases in their priorities, they all filled essentially the same role for the organization in maintaining and moderately growing the business, and all followed a similar dictatorial style whereby the chairman ruled with an iron fist and was not to be argued with. However, as we have seen, the seeds of the downfall of Marks & Spencer were sown plentifully during these reigns. Not only did the accoutrements of success serve to soften the determination of the organization and lead to complacency creeping into the company, but the company became concerned more with its place and role in society, which began to be perceived more and more as a right than a temporary privilege. Successive chairmen, from the Sieffs to Greenbury, spent a large amount of time away from the business pursuing political gratification. Although this paid dividends in terms of title and privilege, with Israel and Marcus Sieff both receiving life peerages, as did Derek Rayner, and Richard Greenbury receiving a knighthood, their political activity undoubtedly took some of their attention away from the business of running Marks & Spencer.

Transformer: Luc Vandevelde (Chairman, 2000–present)

In the short period between chairmen at Marks & Spencer, Peter Salsbury was the chief executive officer, and Brian Baldock, one of the directors, was serving as an interim, non-executive chairman, while for the first time the company searched outside the company for its leader, as companies often need to do when seeking a Transformer. As we have seen, Transformers need to be able to radically change the processes and behavior of the organization while at the same time bring in a new vision for the organization to point the way forward. Failure to do either of these things is likely to result in the failure of the turnaround, particularly if drastic changes and cuts are made without a new vision for the organization which can leave its spirit decimated and without the stomach for drastic change. Unfortunately for Marks & Spencer, this is exactly what happened in this interim period under Salsbury, as he made radical changes in the organization, but without providing a new vision. During this time, Salsbury made some drastic changes to the company, including three restructurings within a few months, firing numerous long-time senior employees, and brutally severing the links with several of Marks & Spencer's largest and long-time suppliers, as he moved belatedly to offshore production. However, while drastic change was necessary, given the state of the company, the axe Salsbury wielded also destroyed much of the spirit and trust that had characterized the company for so long. As sales staff in the stores began to feel unsure of the future and bitter about the way changes were being made, this had a direct impact on customer service, and sales declined even more. Emphasizing the need for a new vision as well as drastic change in a turnaround, one director said of Salsbury's regime:

> Peter had absolutely no vision for the future. In a situation like that he needed to map out the future. He needed to say: "This is where we are going. It will take three years; here are the steps we need to achieve that; there will be pain along the way, but it will be worth it – are you with me?" But there was none of that. When we asked about the future, all Peter could talk about was survival.[22]

It was into this downward spiral that Luc Vandevelde was brought in as chairman in February 2000. Not only was Vandevelde the first outsider to be brought in to head the company, but he was also not British and had no experience in clothing retailing. Vandevelde, a native of Belgium, had spent much of his career at Kraft Foods, working both in the U.S. and Europe. However, in 1995 he became chairman of the French supermarket group Promodès, and transformed it into one of the best performing food groups in France, multiplying the company's value sixfold during his tenure before merging with food giant, Carrefour.

Vandevelde came with a very clear mandate to turn around Marks & Spencer. In May 2000, he stated:

> By the end of the calendar year I would hope we will have a clear demonstration of an improved performance driving the top line. I am very confident we will see rapid improvement in profitability as well. If these results do not come I won't be sitting here in two years' time.[23]

Vandevelde did not waste any time in beginning his turnaround. He hired Roger Holmes as head of UK retailing to revitalize the stores. Holmes had been a consultant with McKinsey & Co, and then worked for retail group Kingfisher where he ran Woolworth and transformed B&Q, Kingfisher's do-it-yourself chain. Within a few months, Salsbury was out as CEO, with Vandevelde assuming the CEO title along with the chairmanship. Vandevelde and Holmes recruited George Davies, who had launched the Next clothing chain, and subsequently the George line of clothing sold through Asda, to launch a fashionable new line called Per Una at Marks & Spencer.

Vandevelde not only curtailed overseas expansion, but extricated M&S from its current overseas operations, selling or closing all 38 stores in mainland Europe, and selling Brooks Brothers in the U.S. Domestically, however, Vandevelde invested in refurbishing the UK stores which had grown tired and dreary. He sold some non-retail investment property that M&S owned, and then, in a fundamental shift for M&S, went into a sale and leaseback arrangement for the retail stores, enabling him to restructure the balance sheet and return £2 billion to shareholders. A year after beginning this turnaround, Vandevelde, like many Transformers, noted how these changes in essence represented a return from an organization that had lost its way to the original vision of the organization:

> When I joined I had to face up to the fact that, in recent years, Marks & Spencer had allowed itself to be distracted from its fundamental strengths and values. Many of the initiatives were peripheral, aimed at attracting new customers in the short term, rather than serving our loyal supporters. Meanwhile, we embarked upon an intense programme of change, much of it long overdue. It has been very disruptive but we have learnt from it. ...

Our strategic review also reinforced the importance of the founding principles of this Company, and it is to a contemporary version of these that we are returning.[24]

Despite his optimistic prediction on the speed of the turnaround, improvement was hard to detect after his first full year, with turnover and profits still slightly declining. However, the two-year prediction was not misplaced, with 2002 profits up 31% from 2001, earnings per share up by a third, and a modest increase in the dividend payment. By now, instead of berating Marks & Spencer as a doomed enterprise, the media was proclaiming the turnaround of a beloved retail icon. In proclaiming the success of the turnaround while emphasizing the need to continue to be focused, Vandevelde once again used the annual report to reiterate the task of the Transformer to bring the organization back to its original mission:

Now that we have turned the corner, our task is to secure the recovery and to keep building for our future. There is much to do and we are not complacent. Phase one may be complete, but the plan moves on as we set about growing the business and regaining our leadership in the UK market.

Before we look forward, it is worth reflecting on why the turnaround has been so relatively swift. Yes we have changed our organizational and financial structures. But more importantly, we have tapped into the values and qualities that customers traditionally associated with our brand but which tended to be obscured in recent years. We have succeeded not by inventing a new Marks & Spencer, but by rediscovering the fundamental strengths of the past and making them relevant to the present.[25]

At the annual meeting in July 2002, Vandevelde announced that Roger Holmes would take on the role of CEO beginning September 1, 2002, and that while remaining chairman, Vandevelde himself would transition to a part-time role beginning in January 2003. This reflects the confidence that Vandevelde and the board have that the transformation of Marks & Spencer is on course and it can maintain steady growth, with the leadership role transitioning from Vandevelde as Transformer to Holmes as Sustainer. However, the respected Lex column in the *Financial Times* questioned whether Marks & Spencer had really seen the completion of the Transformer role and consequently whether the transition was being made too soon:

The announcement of [Vandevelde's] plan to step down as chief executive, expected at Wednesday's annual meeting, could be taken two ways. He is either getting out now because the best is over, or he has considerable faith in his successor and the depth of the company's management. ... It would not be unknown for a chief executive to overestimate the impact of his reforms.[26]

Whether the turnaround under Vandevelde's Transformer role is indeed complete, readying the company for another period of sustained performance, or whether Lex's speculation that the transformation is incomplete and the best is already over remains to be seen. If the latter is the case, then Marks & Spencer may again shortly be seeking another Transformer to revive its fortunes.

Notes

1. Bevan, Judi. 2001. *The Rise and Fall of Marks & Spencer*. London: Profile Books, p. 13.
2. Ibid, p. 25.
3. Ibid, p. 30.
4. Ibid, p. 32.
5. Ibid, pp. 23–4.
6. Bookbinder, Paul. 1993. *Simon Marks, Retail Revolutionary*, London: George Weidenfeld & Nicolson.
7. See note 1, p. 19.
8. Ibid, p. 49.
9. Ibid, p. 38.
10. Ibid.
11. Ibid, p. 28.
12. Sieff, Israel. 1985. *The Memoirs of Israel Sieff*. London: George Weidenfeld & Nicolson.
13. See note 1, p. 62.
14. Ibid.
15. Ibid.
16. Ibid, p. 87.
17. Bower, Joseph and Matthews, John. 1994. *Marks & Spencer: Sir Richard Greenbury's Quiet Revolution*. Harvard Business School case # 9-395-054, p. 3.
18. See note 1, p. 88.
19. Ibid, p. 93.
20. Ibid, p. 128.
21. Ibid, pp. 69–70.
22. Ibid, p. 215.
23. Holinger, Peggy. 2000. M&S chief to resign if sales do not rise. *Financial Times*, May 24.
24. Vandevelde, Luc. 2001. Chairman's Statement. *Marks & Spencer Annual Report to Shareholders*.
25. Ibid.
26. Lex column – Marks & Spencer. *Financial Times*, 8 July, 2002.

Matching Leaders to Evolving Organizations

Having put forward the concept of the Leadership Lifecycle – how organizations go through tangible phases of their existence which require different leadership roles if they are to be navigated successfully – what remains is how to translate this concept into practical applications for individuals and organizations. While some of the lessons for those appointing leaders, individuals seeking leadership roles, and particularly for those currently in leadership roles can be derived from the description of the Leadership Lifecycle itself, it is perhaps worth highlighting the practical applications for each group. The value of the Leadership Lifecycle can be addressed to four primary groups; those aspiring to a leadership position, those currently in a leadership position, those who appoint leaders for organizations, and those who are responsible for developing leaders in their organization.

Lessons for Aspiring Leaders

The key lesson for an aspiring leader is to be aware of your own character and strengths, and to choose an organization to work for which will enable you to best utilize these strengths. The vital element for the progression of an aspiring leader is the fit between the person and the organization. From the descriptions of the various leadership roles, you have probably been able to identify with one or more of the roles as fitting your character. Creators are comfortable dealing with ambiguity, living under uncertainty, and are able to deal with this by having a clear vision of where they are headed and how they want to change the status quo. Accelerators thrive on change and rapid growth, yet have an orientation towards bringing order to the surrounding chaos, thinking systematically about processes which allow for growth. Sustainers prefer order and stability, constantly seeking incrementally better ways of doing things, but remain attuned to their changing environment, willing to adapt vision and process as necessary. Transformers are masters of paradox, able to remain detached, keeping nothing sacred, willing to make whatever change is necessary, but deeply involved in committing to a new vision, or restoring the original vision for the organization. Terminators are able to bring closure to an organization in its current form, and maintain trust and credibility while guiding an organization through a period of uncertainty.

Another clue to the fit between you and the organization comes from looking at the culture of the organization and how it matches your personality and particularly your values. While organizational cultures vary enormously, and the values of the organization are often a reflection of those of the founder or current leaders, there may be some cultural attributes which tend to align with the stage of the lifecycle that the organization is in. Entrepreneurial companies in the Creation stage tend to be more fluid and chaotic and so tend to have a less formal culture, and are willing to adapt quickly to changing circumstances. Creation stage companies are also most likely to have a culture that is a direct reflection of the personality and values of the Creator entrepreneur leading the company. Often these are very strong personalities and result in very strong cultures centered on the personality of the Creator. As such, the cultural variation within companies in the Creation stage tends to be greater than for the later lifecycle stages.

Organizations in the Growth phase are very aggressive in pursuit of growth and evangelizing the market, and this tends to be reflected in the organization's culture. As a consequence, these cultures are often very results oriented and assertive. Taken to extremes, these cultures can be self-destructive as is evident in the Enron scandal where ethical corners were cut in the pursuit of growth. However, these extremes need not be reached if guided by principled leadership from the top. Also, as the organization grows and moves towards the Maturity phase, the increased order and the established systems tend to shift the culture to a more formalized code of conduct, tempering the aggressive nature of the organization.

Organizations in the Maturity phase of the lifecycle tend to have more formal cultures than those in the Creation and Growth phases. Procedures are well established and behaviors are guided by both a formal code and a well-developed informal folklore, where well-known tales of incidents in the organization's past reflect its values and provide a guide to the expected behavior of organizational members. As for the organization as a whole, cultures of organizations in the Maturity phase are well developed and relatively stable, and have been refined slowly over time. As such, they are less susceptible to being a direct reflection of the personalities of the current leadership, although often the Sustainer leader of these organizations has grown up in the company and his or her values and personality are usually fairly congruent with that of the organization itself. Jim Kelly reflects how this is the case at UPS:

> One of our chairmen, George Lamb, used to tell a story I like a lot. He was at some business conference on ethics, and folks were talking about how their companies sometimes forced them to compromise their values – not to tell the customer the whole truth, or to cut corners here or there, or perhaps not report things as openly as they should. When George spoke up, he said his experience had been the opposite: that working at UPS had strengthened his values, made him more honest, and built his integrity. He would tell you that the culture influenced what he did and what he was more than he influenced the culture. And most of us who've been here for a while believe that. So yes, I think the place routinely creates a lot of folks like me.[1]

The corollary of this is that when a leader comes in from the outside and wishes to make substantial changes to the culture of the organization, he or she often meets stiff resistance to change and discovers that mature cultures change very slowly.

Organizations in decline are often susceptible to highly political cultures. Before the organization even realizes that it is in decline, the culture is often characterized by a sense of self-righteousness and complacency as regards the outside world, and an increasingly political battlefield internally as individuals vie for advancement in a static or declining organization and departments contend for political power within the organization. As the organizational decline becomes apparent, blame-shifting tends to divide the company into increasingly separate silos or fiefdoms based around the way the organization is structured, be it by functional area, or by product division, and so forth. Each area tends to become increasingly isolated from the others as it attempts to isolate itself from the effects of decline, shifting blame for the decline on other parts of the organization. This descent of organizational culture into a dysfunctional culture exacerbates the decline of the organization and is often sustained in organizations that eventually collapse. However, the fundamental challenge of the Transformer role is to shift the culture back to a functional culture that supports the revitalized vision for the organization. In the course of this shift, the prevailing culture needs to be fundamentally broken and reformed around values that promote the changes which are occurring in the organization. Thus the culture goes through a period of flux when norms and expected behaviors are reset and the old norms are purged and the new culture created.

While any given company at a particular point in its lifecycle will have a dominant culture, substructures within the company, such as divisions or departments, may be at a different point in their sub-lifecycle and as a result have a different subculture and present an opportunity for using a different leadership role than the one governing the company overall. For example, a division in a mature company that is charged with developing a new product needs a leader in the Creator role to get that product off the ground. Often, if the product is a substantial departure from the core product of the organization, the company may find that isolating the new team in a start-up environment is most effective for developing the breakthroughs it is looking for. In which case, the organization needs to look for a Creator to carry the project forward.

Looking at sub-lifestages within the substructures of an organization may provide you with opportunities for leadership in a wider variety of companies, particularly if you fit best in the Creator leadership role, but it may also limit your progress within a given company, if the leadership role you develop does not fit the current or future lifestage of the overall company. Natural Creators often find life frustrating in large organizations if they can't continually find new ideas that the company is willing to develop.

Lessons for Leaders

If you are currently in a leadership role in an organization, you should be aware of the lifestage that your organization and/or department is in, and conscious of how your own leadership role matches the needs of the organization in this lifestage. The Leadership Lifecycle model offered in this book may have made more visible the match between the lifestage of the organization and your leadership role, and how your strengths contribute to the organization.

The most crucial lessons for leaders from the Leadership Lifecycle model are to be aware of the danger points when an organization is transitioning from one lifestage to the next, and the dangers of extremes of the leadership role. As a leader you need to be aware of the signs that the organization is entering a transition from one phase to the next. As sales begin to pour in and the rudimentary systems of the Creation phase begin to break down, or cash flow begins to tighten even though sales are increasing rapidly, then the organization is beginning its transition from the Creation to the Growth phase. As growth begins to slow to single or low double-digit rates from much higher rates, as the need to hire personnel drops to a manageable rate, and routines are well developed and refined, the company is making the transition from the Growth to the Maturity phase. If signs begin to arise that the organization is not learning and is becoming more inward-looking and insular rather than constantly monitoring its environment, if sales or profits begin to slip and the blame is externalized, then the organization is in danger of slipping from Maturity into Decline. In recognizing these signs, you need to be aware of how the leadership role needs to change to align with the new phase of the organization. As was discussed in Chapter 7, the temptation for leaders, and the worst thing they can do, is to continue in the old leadership role. Indeed, if leaders do this, they tend to go to the extreme of the role, trying to overcompensate for their declining success. However, their diminished success is not due to their skills in that role declining, but rather that the needs of the organization have shifted and the leadership role that had previously matched the organization's needs has become dysfunctional for the organization and, if continued, can lead to the decline or even destruction of the organization.

As was also mentioned in Chapter 7, these transition or danger points for the organization are also present when we see more turnover in the leadership of the organization. While some of this is involuntary, if leaders persist in their old role and organizational performance declines as a result, much of it is also voluntary, as leaders intuitively recognize their strengths and the organizational lifestage to which their strengths best fit. As such, when the organization begins to transition from one lifestage to the next, you as a leader need to make an assessment as to whether you are willing and able to transition to the next leadership role, or whether you can better utilize your strengths by moving to another organization that is in, or transitioning to, the lifestage that corresponds to your preferred leadership role. If you are unwilling or unable to make the transition to the next leadership role, it is much better for you and the organization to move to another opportunity while the fit is still there, or get help in making the transition, rather than waiting until performance becomes dysfunctional. Too often, we observe boards being forced to remove leaders who have stayed in the same leadership role, while the organization has transitioned to the next lifestage, at a considerable cost to both the organization and the ousted leader.

If you are the leader of a sub-unit of the organization, such as a division or department, there is the added complexity of needing to be aware of both the lifecycle stage of your area as well as that of the organization as a whole. Lifecycles of sub-units may move at a different pace to that of the overall organization, and thus transitions in lifestage and the corresponding leadership role may occur earlier and more frequently in the sub-unit than they do in the overall organization. As a leader of a sub-unit you need to be aware of this alignment between the unit's pace through the lifecycle and the pace of the organization and what it means for you as you progress through the organization. Although this may provide the opportunity for experience in different leadership roles in different lifestages within the same organization, ultimately, if you are not comfortable assuming the leadership role that the organization as a whole requires now or in the future, then your career opportunities within the organization may be limited, and at some point you may be best served by looking outside your current organization.

Lessons for Boards

As the board guides the organization through the course of its lifecycle, it is essential that they make use of the concept of the Leadership Lifecycle as they ultimately have responsibility for ensuring a fit between the leader and the leadership needs of the organization. It is critical that as a board member you are aware of the lifestage the organization is in and when it is about to transition into the next phase of the lifecycle. Equally important is that you are able to assess the strengths of the leader and their match to the needed leadership role in the organization. Obviously, this is particularly true when the organization is transitioning from one lifestage to the next, as consecutive leadership roles can be very different from one another and it is far from certain that the leader will be able to effectively transition from one role to the next, even if he or she is prepared to try to make the transition.

The Leadership Lifecycle provides a framework which should make it easier for boards to rationally assess the organization and its leaders and make changes if necessary. Often boards may think that as they went through substantial due diligence in their initial selection of the leader, and that person has been successful in leading the organization forward, they have no reason to doubt the leader's abilities as the organization changes. However, as the Leadership Lifecycle demonstrates, it is not the leader's abilities that need to be questioned, so much as his or her current fit with the changing needs of the organization as it transitions from one phase to the next in the lifecycle.

It is particularly important for board members of organizations in the Maturity phase to be aware of the signals of decline and the possible need to turn to the outside for a new leader. As organizations begin to decline, it is easy to blame small performance dips on some temporary external cause. However, board members must decide whether the causes of the decline are external and temporary, or a failure of the organization to adapt to changing circumstances. If the latter proves to be the case, and the leadership of the organization appears to be growing a sense of heroic self-concept, unwilling to respond to external changes, then it is the board's responsibility to step in and force change on the organization by replacing the leadership with one more appropriate for the new phase of the organization's life.

The board also has ultimate responsibility for ensuring that the leadership talent within the organization goes beyond a single person and there is a leadership depth that is developed. This not only ensures that the organization is being well led at all levels, but also reduces the need for it to look elsewhere for new leadership talent when a need arises. Occasionally, firms may have a strategic reason for going outside the firm for leadership talent, such as when they find themselves in a rapidly changing environment, driven either by technological or environmental change. In these cases, the relevant knowledge changes rapidly, and some firms may decide always to buy talent with current knowledge rather than providing the continual investment to develop that knowledge within the organization. When the underlying environment that the organization exists within changes drastically and permanently, for example for a firm in an industry that is going through deregulation and facing new competitive threats, the board may seek a leader from outside who is used to working in a similar competitive environment. In such cases, the board may strategically choose to go outside rather than attempt to develop talent internally. However, for most companies, it is much more desirable to develop their next generation of leadership talent within the organization than to rely on purchasing it on the open market when the need arises. Developing internal talent provides a continuity of leadership within the organization with in-depth knowledge of the firm-specific challenges and strengths to take the organization forward without punctuated disruptions occurring when leadership changes become necessary.

Lessons for Leadership Development

Leadership development is critical to almost all organizations. How it is done, and who does it, sends a very strong signal both internally and externally as to the belief the organization has in its people and its future. And the tone is set by the current leaders of the organization. Larry Bossidy, an executive with General Electric for 34 years, a firm highly regarded for its ability to produce leaders, left GE in 1991 to take over as CEO of AlliedSignal. Bossidy brought with him a heavy emphasis on developing leaders, and saw it lacking at AlliedSignal:

> When I joined AlliedSignal as CEO, one of my first acts was to visit plants, meet the managers, and get a feel for their individual capabilities. In the course of these meetings, I realized that the company's inattention to leadership development was a major problem.[2]

In order to correct this problem and get the message to his managers of its importance to the company, he realized that he had to make it his highest priority, despite the other urgent matters that clamored for his attention:

> I devoted what some people considered an inordinate amount of emotional energy and time – perhaps between 30% and 40% of my day for the first two years – to hiring and developing leaders. That's a huge amount of time for a CEO to devote to any single task. It wasn't easy to hold that discipline, especially when you consider that I'd inherited a company whose investors, analysts, suppliers, customers and top executives all cried out for attention. But I knew it was essential. I'm convinced that AlliedSignal's success was due in large part to the amount of time and emotional commitment I devoted to leadership development. …
>
> Many executives have neglected a personal involvement, accountability, and initiative in developing leaders within their organizations. But because it is full of unknowns, of unpredictability, it deserves more time than anything else you do as CEO.[3]

The Leadership Lifecycle can be used by organizations to inform and structure the development of leaders, and this development can be approached with two primary philosophies: nurturing specialists or developing generalists. By understanding the nature of the organization's lifecycle and how it transitions between phases, together with an understanding of the corresponding leadership role requirements, organizations can choose to develop leaders either with a specialist depth in a particular leadership role, or broaden their experience, challenging them across multiple leadership roles and thereby developing generalists. Virtually all large organizations, and many smaller ones, have departments, divisions, or product offerings which are at a different phase of the life-cycle than the organization as a whole. Therefore it needs leaders to take on roles that are not the same as the role at the head of the organization, and can use these opportunities to train the next generation of leaders. There are pros and cons to both of these development strategies, and it is pertinent that an organization be aware of these to enable a conscious decision on which option best fits the needs of the organization.

By using the lifecycle model to develop leaders who are specialists in one particular type of role, the organization gains the benefit of nurturing leaders with expertise in a particular role, resulting in a more predictable performance. The organization can work with the individual, based on the individual's strengths and personality, to ensure that the fit between the individual and the leadership role they engage in is optimally matched for both the individual and the organization. Consequently, this approach also enables the organization to attract and retain people with strengths in leadership roles that do not match the current lifestage of the overall organization, but are still necessary within the sub-units of the organization to enable it to grow, for example by bringing Creators into mature organizations to focus on new product development. The potential downside to this approach is that the organization's succession planning needs to be able to ensure that there are continually places requiring that leadership role in order to retain the individual as they progress through the organization. Equally, for the individual, if the role expertise that the individual develops is not the one that fits the overall lifestage of the organization, there may be limited opportunities and the organization risks other organizations poaching these leaders they develop.

Developing generalist leadership skills by deliberately rotating its next generation of leaders through assignments in sub-units at different lifestages, requiring different leadership roles, enables the organization to prepare leaders for all eventualities that the organization faces. Particularly if the organization is in a single business, rather than spread across multiple businesses, this approach allows the organization to develop leaders who have a thorough understanding of the entire business, developing sensitivity to how strategic business decisions will affect the whole organization. The potential cost of this development approach, however, is that because the leadership roles at the various lifestages are so different from one another, and require different skills of the individual, individuals are more prone to failing, or underperforming, at one or more of the roles as they rotate through the organization. Particularly if these next generation leaders are given substantial profit-and-loss responsibility in these assignments, underperforming could have a negative effect on the organization as a whole and on the individual leader's reputation and confidence. How the organization views and deals with leaders who are very good at one or two of the roles, but underperform in others is critical to the success of this approach to leadership development. It is a very unusual leader who can excel at all the leadership roles, and so the organization needs to be aware of this and have ways of utilizing the strengths of their leaders and limiting the downside risk, while still developing leaders who understand the entire organization.

Whether the organization takes the generalist or specialist approach to developing the next generation of leaders, organizations can benefit from using the Leadership Lifecycle to develop talent at all points on the lifecycle. The approach it takes depends on the preference, strategy, and goals of the organization. But the organization's long-term survival requires that, whatever approach it takes, it heeds the lessons of the Leadership Lifecycle.

Notes

1. Kirby, Julia. 2001. Reinvention with respect. An interview with Jim Kelly of UPS. *Harvard Business Review*, November, pp. 116–23, p. 120.
2. Bossidy, Larry. 2001. The job no CEO should delegate. *Harvard Business Review*, March, pp. 5–7, p. 6.
3. Ibid, p. 5, 7.